"If you are not an assertive person, this book will help you. It is a down-to-earth, practical and eminently sensible guide to achieving successful interactions with all the people in your life – inside and outside the workplace."
Professor Brenda Gourley, Former Vice Chancellor and CEO of The Open University

"Written in a down-to-earth and pragmatic style, this book shows that asserting yourself in the right way will lead to a happier, more satisfying and healthy life and bring profound rewards at work and home – a great read!"
Simon Cooper, Director of Organisation Effectiveness at Informatica Corporation and Author of *Brilliant Leader*

"We all sometimes hit low points in our lives and careers. I loved this book as it was brilliant at reminding me of the importance to prepare and practice for those challenging situations that we face at work and at home."
Donna Kinnair DBE, Chief Nurse NHS Southeast London

"Whether at home, at work, at rest or at play, being assertive can be the difference between getting what you want and failing to meet your own standards. This book shows how to be yourself and improve your life by saying what needs to be said."
David Holdgate, CEO, Satellite Information Services

"Getting the right balance of assertiveness is critical, especially in your career – this book is an empowering, practical guide in how to achieve this."
Gary Bullard, CEO, Logica, UK

"The perfect read for anyone who wants to be more assertive in any area of their life."
Ann Craven, Director Supply Chain, Invensys

"In this book, Conrad and Suzanne bring their wisdom, experience and unique viewpoints to bear on one of the most challenging areas of human interaction."
John Varney, CEO, Maximum Clarity

"A practical and down-to-earth guide showing you how to be more assertive; it will help you, friends, family and colleagues communicate better and get more from life."
Stella Collins, MD, Stellar Learning & Founder of The Brain Friendly Learning Group

"*Assertiveness* provides open, honest and practical solutions to help you communicate your ideas clearly and get what you want when it really matters"
Kevin Davidson, CEO, Maxwell Drummond International

"This book is an empowering, practical guide to transforming your life by becoming more assertive."
Simon Vyvyan, CEO, Industry Media Ltd

"This book shares a wealth of sound practical advice to help you be more assertive, effective and in control of your life."
Sally Morris, Housing Manager, Littlehampton & Rustington Housing Society

"Read this book and you can pull even the hardest people into line. As a manager, you need your team to be on board with you and deliver projects – this book will put you on the path to project success."
Clive Davies, Project Manager, Engineering, Metadata

Assertiveness

How to be strong in every situation

Conrad & Suzanne Potts

CAPSTONE

Cover design: Binary & The Brain

© 2013 Conrad & Suzanne Potts

Registered office

Capstone Publishing Ltd. (A Wiley Company), John Wiley and Sons Ltd, The Atrium, Southern Gate, Chichester, West Sussex, PO19 8SQ, United Kingdom

For details of our global editorial offices, for customer services and for information about how to apply for permission to reuse the copyright material in this book please see our website at www.wiley.com.

The right of the author to be identified as the author of this work has been asserted in accordance with the Copyright, Designs and Patents Act 1988.

Wiley publishes in a variety of print and electronic formats and by print-on-demand. Some material included with standard print versions of this book may not be included in e-books or in print-on-demand. If this book refers to media such as a CD or DVD that is not included in the version you purchased, you may download this material at http://booksupport.wiley.com. For more information about Wiley products, visit www.wiley.com.

Designations used by companies to distinguish their products are often claimed as trademarks. All brand names and product names used in this book and on its cover are trade names, service marks, trademark or registered trademarks of their respective owners. The publisher and the book are not associated with any product or vendor mentioned in this book. None of the companies referenced within the book have endorsed the book.

Limit of Liability/Disclaimer of Warranty: While the publisher and author have used their best efforts in preparing this book, they make no representations or warranties with the respect to the accuracy or completeness of the contents of this book and specifically disclaim any implied warranties of merchantability or fitness for a particular purpose. It is sold on the understanding that the publisher is not engaged in rendering professional services and neither the publisher nor the author shall be liable for damages arising herefrom. If professional advice or other expert assistance is required, the services of a competent professional should be sought.

Library of Congress Cataloging-in-Publication Data is available

A catalogue record for this book is available from the British Library.

ISBN 978–0-857–08368–5 (paperback) ISBN 978–0-857–08366–1 (ebk)
ISBN 978–0-857–08367–8 (ebk) ISBN 978–0-857–08365–4 (ebk)

Set in 10/13.5 pt Sabon by Toppan Best-set Premedia Limited

Printed in Great Britain by TJ International Ltd, Padstow, Cornwall, UK

This book is dedication to our children Sarah, Jo & Oliver

Contents

Introduction

Assertion is more than just a set of techniques – it is a way of thinking about how to be authentic and get the most from life. Assertion is supported by beliefs which develop a positive mental approach to life's ups and downs. You become the puppeteer and not the puppet.

Almost everyone seems to be working under greater pressure as the demands of the job or life in general increase. Life changes, such as moving house, getting married or coping with bereavement, can further contribute to this pressure.

We know demands come from various sources, both from things occurring in our external environment as well as what's occurring internally – in our heads, we all know how our mind affects us physically too.

The internal pressures may be products of how comfortable and pleased you are with yourself, your body, what you say to yourself, aspects of your personality, life experiences, your belief systems, your sense of self-worth and purpose.

We use assertive behavioural skills to achieve a greater balance between competing demands, so that you can learn how to experience less stress, become better at managing your time, be more satisfied with how you behave and, in turn, lead a really happy, healthy and fulfilling existence.

We see assertiveness helping you excel in all the areas of your life, be it social, spiritual, financial, at work or with your family. What happens around you is often a reflection of your own creation. Your thinking determines the results you get. Think negatively and you will attract negative realities; think assertively and the benefits of life will come to you.

As training consultants, specializing in the field of assertion for the last 30 years, we have been privileged to run assertiveness training programmes across the globe: in Europe, the emerging democracies of Eastern Europe, Asia, the South Pacific and the Middle East. We've managed to help literally thousands of people stand up for their views and ideas and achieve more wealth, health and happiness.

We have been invited to conduct assertiveness training at all levels within organizations to change and develop more cooperative business cultures.

Increasingly, we have engaged with CEOs and chairmen of boards, and have been part of British industry's drive to develop more women to board-level positions.

Our keynote speaking for industry conferences, corporate events, education seminars and charity forums has encouraged participants to revitalize their approach both at work and at home.

In Part One of this book we explore the characteristics of assertion and a range of assertive behavioural tools to use.

Then, in Part Two, we describe a variety of real-life situations that you will no doubt have some experience of. We'll take the assertive principles discussed in Part One into a number of challenging social and work situations. We will demonstrate how you can put into practice these assertive tools, within these various settings, so that you build your self-confidence and esteem, and get more of what you want by paying attention to what others want.

Throughout the book there are a number of exercises for you to complete, to reinforce your learning and have some fun experimenting.

Since you've chosen to read this book we acknowledge that you're investing in your future. Thank you for setting aside the time to do this, and we wish you a very satisfying and rewarding life.

Seize the day – the journey of a thousand miles begins with the first step.

Horace/Lao-tse

Conrad & Suzanne Potts

PART ONE

1
What is Assertion?

What is Assertion?

There are many definitions of the word assertion. Indeed, people often attend assertiveness training to get more of their own way or to be more forceful.

Our view is that assertion is about something quite different:

Assertiveness is a behaviour that seeks to achieve a win-win – a satisfactory outcome for both parties.

When you adopt assertive behaviour you get more of what you want, but only when you acknowledge and give consideration to what the other person wants or needs. It's the paradox of win-win that makes it possible.

If you want to be a success in your personal life, business, career, or anything you choose to mention, you need to be assertive in your communication and take responsibility for your life.

Assertive people are successful because they are considered as authentic, "what you see is what you get," straight shooters who you can rely on to be honest and forthright – you know where you stand.

Behaving more assertively will increase your happiness in life and you are likely to have a longer life span than someone who is communicating aggressively or passively.

Assertion gives you permission to state your needs clearly and allows you to ask others to acknowledge them. Assertion requires you to listen to others' needs and to acknowledge them.

You need a number of tools and resources to maintain your confidence, feel strong yet flexible, trust in your abilities and work in ways that bring you enjoyment and pleasure in what you do. You need to know you are not a prisoner of events or circumstances and that you can positively influence and change the world in which you live.

We believe behaving assertively helps you achieve this and so much more. Behaving in an assertive way allows you to focus, and to achieve what is possible, rather than preoccupying yourself with doubt, misgivings and focusing on what you think is not possible.

Three ways of behaving

We can behave in any of three ways:

- aggressively
- non-assertively (sometimes called passive aggression)
- assertively.

We are not our behaviours, even if we are sometimes described as such. No one behaves assertively, aggressively or non-assertively all the time.

People vary their behaviour between all three and are more likely to react aggressively or non-assertively when they feel under pressure or stressed.

There may be certain situations in which you find it more difficult to be assertive, or people who are more difficult to be assertive with. Your assertive behaviour may break down at work, at home or when you are out with friends. It may happen more often with certain types of people e.g. those in authority, people you think are smarter or more competent than you, relatives, or members of the opposite sex.

All three behaviours work and that is why we keep repeating them.

1. Aggression

Aggressive behaviour is when you:

- Stand up for your own rights in such a way that you violate the rights of another.
- Express your thoughts, feelings and beliefs in unsuitable and inappropriate ways, even though you may honestly believe those views to be right.

Aggression enhances your own position at the expense of others and can be used to put another person down. Aggression is based on the belief that your opinions are more important than other people's. It is characterized by blaming other people or outside factors, by showing contempt, and being hostile, attacking or patronizing.

Aggression can sometimes be confused with assertion.

If someone communicates in an aggressive way, such as raising their voice, staring people down, or constantly interrupting, others may remain quiet and acquiescent and give in. The aggression can be perceived as confidence: "you really told them there!" – with such feedback reinforcing the idea that this behaviour is assertive.

If you have been non-assertive and compliant and held back your emotions the dam may burst and you decide, "that's it – enough is enough – no more."

You may, in the first instance, overstep the mark and express all the pent-up emotion by demanding your rights, insisting your needs be met *now*, and communicating in an aggressive way.

If this behaviour succeeds, where your non-assertion in the past did not, this "success," this new-found power, may seduce you into thinking you are being assertive.

A good example of this was John, who came on one of our assertiveness programmes. After the first day he was so impressed with the material and his new-found assertive skills, he decided to go out for dinner and practise what he had learned from day 1 of the programme.

John pitched up the next day looking all forlorn and thoroughly dejected.

The programme hadn't properly kicked in yet, and I asked him if he'd enjoyed his evening out and whether he had any chance yet to put his new-found learning to use.

"This assertiveness doesn't work for me," he said. "I tried it last night and it was a complete failure. I'm one of those guys who goes in to a crowded bar, shuffles up to the front and tries to order a drink. Invariably I am the very last person served even though other people have arrived long after me.

"It's not only in pubs but also in restaurants, where I'll be the last one to get served despite being there before others.

"Last night I thought I'd change all that. I remembered all that you said about body language, voice control and using assertive language, and it still didn't work.

"I sat down at my table and tried to engage the waitress as she walked by, but she never stopped at my table. She handed out menus to everyone but me; even people who came long after me got the menu first.

"After 10 minutes or so I had had enough. As the waitress walked by I gently held out my hand, stared her down and said, 'Excuse me Miss, but I've been waiting here for about 15 minutes and you've handed out the menu to everyone but me. This is making me very annoyed and unless I get my menu straight away and my food even quicker I am going to leave.'

"And you know what? She turned round and said 'I'm sorry you're disappointed, sir, but it is your prerogative to do what you want.'

"So I did. I got up and walked out."

Although John stood up for his needs in no uncertain manner his first interaction with his waitress was hostile and threatening and it was no wonder the conversation resulted in a failure.

"She is very assertive," people say, "I wouldn't mess with her or get in her way." "He's very assertive and always gets what he wants no matter what."

When you adopt this behaviour, sometimes you get what you want and, at other times, you will invite opposition and dislike.

Society and some cultures reward aggressive behaviour. Those who are aggressive can succeed. As with assertion, aggression can represent standing up for yourself and your views but at the expense of others. Others seem to admire you for your strength, confidence, and commitment – provided they are not at the receiving end!

2. Non-assertion
Non-assertive behaviour is when you:

- fail to stand up for your rights or do so in such a way that other people can easily disregard them;
- express your thoughts, feelings and beliefs in apologetic, cautious or self-effacing ways; or
- fail to express your views or feelings altogether.

Submission is based on the belief that your own needs and wants will be seen by others to be less important than their own. Typical examples of submissive behaviour are long, justifying explanations, and putting yourself down whilst attempting to accommodate the needs and views of others.

Non-assertion may appear to be harmless but can equally deny your rights and the opportunity for a win-win. A lack of desire to take responsibility is often the root cause of non-assertive behaviour and can encourage us and others to behave aggressively. It is less dramatic than aggressive behaviour but nevertheless pervasive.

Sandra was an energetic and achievement oriented kind of a lady. She described herself as a "can do" sort of a person, who liked nothing better than to be given an impossible or very difficult job to do, and a straight talker who let people know how she felt.

She expected others to respond in the same way and was often frustrated when they didn't share the same concern, sense of urgency or commitment. If the job demanded she work harder, she did; if she needed to stay later, she did, and she pulled out all the stops to deliver on her and the company's promises.

What Sandra found most frustrating and annoying was the reluctance of her staff to take the initiative. She would approach them and agree a commitment to do a job, only to find out too late that the deadlines were not going to be met. Sandra suspected that, despite their apparent agreement, there never was a real intention to comply.

Sandra would first become frustrated, then angry and then those staff involved would feel the sharpness of her tongue:

"I ask them quite politely: can they do the job, do they know how to do the job and can the job be done in the timescales?

"Everyone says 'yes', I even check – 'are you sure?', and they still say 'yes', so I have to believe them.

"Why don't they say the time is too tight or I don't know how to do it, or I need extra help, I'd be only too willing to support them but they keep their heads down and just say yes? No wonder I lose my temper and am aggressive towards them!"

When you adopt non-assertive behaviour you can be at your most manipulative in order to avoid confrontation, rejection, criticism and even praise.

Non-assertion is based on fear, avoidance and, from our experience, is most damaging to our confidence and self-esteem.

3. Assertion

Assertive behaviour is when you:

- stand up for your own rights in a way that does not violate another person's rights;
- directly express your point of view, say what you want openly and without manipulation; or
- seek to understand and engage with others in a way of genuine mutuality.

It leads to an honest, open and direct expression of our point of view which, at the same time, shows that we understand the other person's position.

Rebecca was a strong-minded individual, definite about what she wanted. She was never one to hold back on her point of view. She was a caring person who listened and spoke in equal measure and was respected for being calm and assured. Such authority and assurance was soon noted and Rebecca found she was repeatedly promoted until she hit the heady heights of the senior management team.

Every Monday morning the team was expected to come in early and take part in the Monday morning meeting to look ahead at the week's opportunities and problems.

Rebecca had to get up extra early to make these meetings, and organize special childcare arrangements as she couldn't take her children to school as she would normally do.

The meetings seemed to have a consistent pattern and, being a newcomer to the team, Rebecca sat back respectfully and observed, participating when appropriate.

The boss would stand up at the start of the meeting and give a 20 minute monologue. He would then invite participation from everyone. The meeting would ramble on directionless, taking as many detours as the number of people who spoke.

Some two hours later, with nothing decided, everyone would shuffle off to their departments to start their morning's work, muttering, and complaining under their breath that the last two hours had been a thorough waste of time.

At the next meeting, after the boss' monologue, Rebecca stood up and calmly asked her boss.

"Brian, I have been to three meetings now and I am not sure what they are trying to achieve. I really want to contribute in a meaningful way and use the time most productively. I feel I can't at the moment so can you set some objectives for these meetings so that I feel it is a good use of my time? And could we put a time limit to it so it's not so open-ended?"

Brian sat back stunned, as if in shock. The rest of the management team waited for Brian's reply, secretly thinking that this had been one of the finest career limiting speeches they had ever witnessed.

To his everlasting credit Brian hauled himself up to his full height and slowly and deliberately thanked Rebecca for her honesty and forthrightness. The meetings had drifted, he admitted, from their original purpose and he carefully crafted three objectives for the meeting. The meeting then proceeded to take an hour to complete.

That wasn't the end of Rebecca's story. If any of the senior managers went to a meeting they would ask, "I'd like to fully participate but don't think I can unless we have specific objectives. What are they?" And when they ran their own meetings they made sure they had objectives.

Soon it became a part of the culture of that organization to ask this question at every meeting.

Consequently, meetings had greater focus, were more satisfying, decision based and took less time. The biggest pay-off, however, was that the number of meetings decreased by a third in that company.

Rebecca continued at the company, her value and respect enhanced.

Recognizing the three behaviours

Each of the three behavioural types, aggression, non-assertion and assertion, encapsulate a different way of perceiving the world, a different world view.

Let us look at the world view and language patterns of each behavioural type.

Aggression

World view

The world is a hostile place, and the only way to survive is to be stronger and display strength – there are no medals for losers – strike first, the best defence is attack – my needs are important, not so sure about yours.

Best summarized by "I win, you lose."

Language patterns

- Attacking: "Only *you* could think of something like that!"
- Excessive use of and overemphasis on "I" and "my" statements: "*I'd* like it done *my* way in future because *I'm* paying the bill."
- Expressing opinion as fact: "The world's a dangerous place and it's always going to be like it."
- Exclusive focus on your needs and disregarding others: "I need it done now so you need to get on with it straight away."
- Blaming: "It's your fault we're in this mess, I said no good would come of it but you wouldn't listen."
- Threatening: "If you don't do that right I can guarantee that I'll have to take measures you won't like."
- Excessive use of "ought," "must," "should": "You must appreciate that we should do it this way – it's something we all ought to do."
- Exaggeration: "Everybody would agree that we all need everything in order before we start."
- Denigrating: "Only a fool would think that could possibly be acceptable."
- Manipulating: "If you really cared for me you wouldn't leave me alone like this."

Non-Assertion

World view

I am not important, my views, needs and wants are not as important as those of other people. I am fearful and anxious about standing up for my needs etc., and if I do stand up for them I am likely to do so in a way that makes it easy for others to override or ignore them. I can stand up for them, however, by being manipulative or making others feel guilty or sorry for me.

Best summarized by "I lose, you win" or "if I lose, you lose too!"

Language patterns

- Tentative and reluctant agreement: "Well maybe I can try."
- Hinting at doubts: "Well I don't know if that's the right thing to do, what would others say?"
- Unwilling to state a preference: "We could go out, or we could stay in or maybe we could get a take away? What do you think?"
- Moaning or complaining: "Why me? It always happens to me."
- Fishing: "It's the first time I've done something like this, not very good is it?"
- Seeking permission and approval: "Should I really go ahead and should I just be quiet?"
- Self-pity: "Why is it always me that has to tell the kids off?"
- Self-effacing: "I'm no good at something like this, you do it so much better."
- Suggestions at your expense: "Oh, I've said you would help out tomorrow, I know you wouldn't mind."
- Long, rambling sentences: "Well you know how it is with that lot . . . they come along and ask you for a favour without even considering whether you want to do it or not . . . well, I tried to explain . . . how come they don't know that I can't

drop everything? . . . and that I might need more notice? . . .
well, if they think I'm happy about it they can think again
. . . I suppose I should tell them . . . but then they should
know shouldn't they? I've a good mind to tell them but they
wouldn't listen, would they?"

Assertion

World view

I have needs and wants as do others – I have as much right as others
to express myself – I am responsible for my own behaviour and its
consequences – I can stand up for what I believe without attacking
others – I don't have to lose so that others can win. I can ask for
what I need, want etc., openly and honestly.

Best summarized by "win, win."

Language patterns

- Ownership of ideas, views and feelings: "This is how I see
  the situation . . ." "In my opinion/view we need to tackle this
  first." "When I find myself in this situation I feel hesitant and
  cautious when putting forward my point of view."
- Stating what you want: "What I'd like/prefer/want/need is to
  do this with you."
- Focus on behaviour and facts instead of opinions: "I thought
  when you cheered and complimented Jill you showed how
  supportive you can be."
- Distinguishing opinion from fact: "In my view that's very
  unfair."
- Clarity: "I don't have a strong preference for either and will
  be genuinely happy whichever one we do."
- Brevity: "What do you think?"

- Questions: Particularly open questions that invite others to give their views, ideas, needs or wants rather than just a "Yes/ No" answer. "What, Why, When, How, Where, Which and Who."
- Focus on what can be done: "I can see how difficult it is, we can take that into consideration and plan for it."

Exercise

There are a number of situations in the following examples 1–9.

You will find three responses which we believe are typical of an aggressive, assertive and non-assertive reply in each situation.

Which option a) b) or c) would you chose? Which one do you think would be likely to:

- Achieve the better result?
- Is the assertive response?

Make a note of your answers and check against ours at the end of the exercise.

Example 1

Imagine you are watching a film at the cinema and some people behind you are chattering away and spoiling your enjoyment as well as others'.

   a) You could turn around and say: "Shut up! Can't you see you're spoiling everyone's enjoyment?"

   b) You could say very loudly to your partner, so that those behind you chattering would hear: "I wish the people behind would speak quieter so we can enjoy the film."

   c) You could say: "Excuse me, would you mind not talking, it makes it very difficult to listen to the film."

(Continued)

21

Example 2

Your boss, at very short notice, asks you to complete a very important report that will mean you working throughout the weekend. You have already arranged to go away with family and friends for the weekend.

You could say:

a) "You know I'd really like to help and usually I am more than happy to oblige – it's only that this weekend isn't very convenient . . . I mean it's a bit short notice and I am not sure if I can really help that much – have you asked anyone else – what have they said?"

b) "Lesley, I understand this is important – normally I am willing to help out in whatever way I can. This weekend I have arranged to go away with the family and won't be able to work on this report. How else can I help?"

c) "You've got quite a problem there but there is no way I am going to alter my plans for the weekend. I suggest you approach someone else."

Example 3

It's at the end of one of those long, hard weeks and you are looking forward to "me" and "us" time. You get a telephone call from a friend asking you over for a Saturday night meal and a bit of a celebration.

You could say:

a) "Thanks for the invite, Nic, I really feel tired after a hard week and would appreciate time relaxing at home. Another time, but not this time."

b) "No, we're doing something else so can't come."

c) "Thanks very much for inviting us. I'm not sure, but I think we may be planning something else that evening, I'd have to check my diary because I have a feeling we have something arranged. Can I call you back later?"

Example 4

A colleague, Sam, asks you for a lift home. It's inconvenient for you as you're late already and the drive will take you out of your way.

You could say:

a) "You know I would if I could, only today is very difficult – I have got a lot of things to do and I said I would be home on time for once – so you see I am not sure I can help you. Maybe if you asked around someone else might be going in your direction – sorry, I hope you're not upset."

b) "I am always going out of my way for you, but not this time."

c) "Sam, I am already late and I want to get home on time today. Another time and I'd be more than willing but not today."

Example 5

Your partner has "volunteered" your help to a neighbour, not for the first time, without first asking you. You are very annoyed.

You could say:

a) "So, you've done it again. You always pick on me to help just because I never complain or make a fuss. It's not right and I think it's very unfair – I suppose I'll have to help this time because now you have said I'll help and everyone will be upset if I don't turn up. It's really not considerate and takes advantage of my easy-going nature."

b) "Please don't volunteer me in future without asking me. I feel very annoyed when you do. I think you need to speak to the neighbours and ask them to speak to me direct."

c) "That's the last time you'll do that without asking me. You make me feel very angry that you just do it and don't bother to find out whether I will or not. Stop it!"

(Continued)

Example 6

Your manager gives you another chunk of work. You already have too much on, and the deadlines for this piece of work are very tight.

You could say:

a) "It's just too much, you can't really expect me to handle all of this – not possible!"
b) "Aubrey, I can't do this work in the timescales you are suggesting. We need to talk further."
c) "Aubrey, thank you. Leave it with me and I will have a look at it and see what I can do."

Example 7

You made a special effort to meet a friend at a particular time. Half an hour later they saunter up to you with a smile on their face.

You could say:

a) "About time! What time do you think this is?"
b) "I thought you were never coming – I thought I'd got the wrong time – the traffic I imagine has been bad."
c) "Jess, I thought we had agreed to meet at 1 o'clock. What happened?"

Example 8

You are ambitious and want to show everyone how competent you are, but the truth is you don't know how to get started on a particular high profile job. Your boss notices your hesitancy and asks if everything is OK.

You could say:

a) "I believe I can make a success of this project but I need help from you just to kick-start it."
b) "It's quite a demanding project, very interesting with a number of different angles to it. I can see there are a number

of different ways of starting it, each of them have their own
'pros' and 'cons' so it's a matter of which one is the best."
c) "Absolutely no problem – I could do a dozen of these before
breakfast."

Example 9
You are at a family gathering and you are enthusiastically defending
the actions of a particular minority group when another family
member says " that's typical of someone like you – you don't know
what you are talking about."

You could say:

a) Nothing, keep quiet and laugh along with everybody else.
b) "What makes you so sure I don't?"
c) "Oh yes I do, I certainly know a hell of a lot more than you!"

Answers 1–9
We are not suggesting that the responses would end or resolve the
situation but the first response you make back can determine the
"climate" or "tone" of the ensuing conversation. When you start
well, you increase the chances of finishing well.

Example 1
a) aggressive; b) non-assertive; c) assertive

Example 2
a) non-assertive; b) assertive; c) aggressive

Example 3
a) assertive; b) aggressive; c) non-assertive

Example 4
a) non-assertive; b) aggressive; c) assertive

(Continued)

25

Example 5
a) non-assertive; b) assertive; c) aggressive

Example 6
a) aggressive; b) assertive; c) non-assertive

Example 7
a) aggressive; b) non-assertive; c) assertive

Example 8
a) assertive; b) non-assertive; c) aggressive

Example 9
a) non-assertive; b) assertive; c) aggressive

All of us behave in all three ways in some situations, and in others we act more aggressively or non-assertively – which of course doesn't mean that we are only aggressive or non-assertive people. Assertion is about behaviour not people.

The aim of this book is to help you increase your assertion in more and more situations where it's appropriate for you to do so.

Now tally up your responses as a simple way of seeing what way you tend to behave most.

Summary

When we behave assertively we are putting our own needs on an equal basis with the needs of others. It is important for our own well-being to do this. This is also helpful for other people since we are not doing anyone a favour by letting them take us for granted or get whatever they want from us.

When you can find a solution that maintains the dignity, respect and needs of others you are more likely to achieve a long lasting result that all parties can sign up to.

Of course this is not always the easy option, it's easier sometimes just to give in or put your foot down and stick to your guns no matter what.

If you want to be happier, healthier, more successful – in whatever terms you define success – you must take greater responsibility for yourself and behave in an inter-dependent way. That could inevitably mean changing your perspective about the world you live in but, more especially, how you perceive yourself.

2
Win-Win

Assertive behaviour is more than a set of techniques. It is an attitude and a belief system about how you want to be treated and how you want to treat others.

A few years ago we were invited by the MD of a sales-focused engineering company to spend a day with his senior team to talk about the "culture" of the company. There was growing evidence that an aggressive approach to winning business was beginning to falter, with revenues declining.

Everything went well on the first morning. We covered a number of techniques they believed to be useful and then we began to explore the fundamentals of "win-win."

It was easy to see why the company had an aggressive model, which was often stimulated by the MD himself. To give him credit he sat through a session on why the company should become more "win win" orientated but, in the end, something must have triggered his frustration.

"All this is OK in theory, and we'd all like to be nice towards our customers, but business is a hard-nosed game where the survival of the fittest is the prime law. It's eat or be eaten and make sure you strike first."

We discussed a number of ways of dealing with customers and these were distilled into four distinct approaches called the Win-Win Corral. I made the argument for each and waited for his response. "Let's imagine," I said, "that we adopted one of these four approaches:"

The win-win corral

1. Win-lose
The approach here is to imagine that, in negotiations, the customer "wins" and the company loses out. Good for customers and customer relations, but is that a sustainable strategy?

31

"That may work short-term," he said "or perhaps as a 'loss-leader', but clearly we'd go out of business before very long, so it's not a strategy where the company could survive long-term."

2. Lose-win

There is another approach: lose-win. Here, you seek an outcome which clearly favours the company but leaves the customer feeling that they have lost out.

"So you could try it the other way round," I suggested, "and act on the basis of lose-win. In this case you'd make lots of money but, in many instances, your customers would probably feel they didn't get value for money and that you were not that concerned about customer care and retention. Would that be a worthwhile approach?"

"Sounds intriguing," he said with a smile, "I hope we aren't perceived as treating our customers that way. We wouldn't last long after their first time visit and it wouldn't promote customer loyalty and long-term sustainability."

3. Lose-lose

Yet another approach is lose-lose. With this strategy, both parties – the customer and the company – feel dissatisfied that they have not got enough of what they want.

"Daft as it may seem," I said, "you could give it a try. You might compromise on a price or service level that you know won't make profit, and yet still have the customer feeling you were charging too much or that they hadn't really got what they wanted. Would that be sustainable?"

This scenario got the shortest response from the MD accompanied by much facial contortion.

"You can't be serious, who in their right mind would do that?"

4. Win-win

The fourth approach is win-win. This strategy is one where both parties feel that they have got sufficient of what they need: the customer feels satisfied they have value for money and the company feels it has sold at a price that meets its needs.

"We do have our last approach," I said, "and it is one where you and the customer believe they have a fair deal and value for money – that there is something in it for them and enough in it for you – a win-win."

"Ideal," he said begrudgingly, "probably the approach that would best achieve long-term customer loyalty, repeat business, growth and long-term sustainability. But it is not easy to accomplish."

"No," I said, "it is probably the most difficult option, but is it worthwhile choosing any other approach?"

Whether you are a company or an individual the same options are open to you in your everyday negotiations with work colleagues, family, friends and any other encounters in your daily life.

What is win-win?

In negotiation terms, to achieve a win-win, both parties should feel sufficiently satisfied with the outcome or result at the end of the negotiation stage.

We negotiate every day of our lives. Perhaps not the kind of negotiation that helps to rebuild nations and cultures. It is more likely to be the everyday, mundane discussion or encounter in which one person wants one thing and the other person another. For example:

- who has control of the remote control,
- who will walk the dog or do the shopping, and
- who will make the dinner or pick up the kids . . .

The ideal situation is where the other person wants what you are prepared to give and that you are prepared to give what the other person wants. But this is not always the case . . .

Whether you are the MD of an engineering company, a high level negotiator, or an individual dealing with everyday situations, you have four basic approaches to get results. (There is also an additional, fifth approach, for when individuals don't want to "play" win-win. This is what we call "no win, no play," and is explained later in this chapter.)

The four main approaches are illustrated in the Win-Win Corral diagram below.

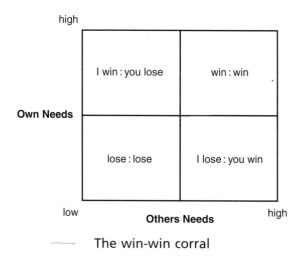

The win-win corral

34

A win-win process

Let us now look at a five-step process to achieve win-win.

Step 1 – Hold assertive beliefs

You first need to *believe* that win-win is possible. This belief enables you to be courageous, considerate and persistent in the search for mutual resolution.

Specific beliefs may be as follows:

* A person's needs may be different . . . they are still valid for that person.
* My needs are important, so are others.
* I don't have to lose, for others to win.
* There is always the potential for a win-win.

Step 2 – Establish your own needs and wants

When stating your needs, be specific. People tend to express what they *want* as opposed to what they really *need* e.g.

* "I want some help doing this," or
* "I need some help for ten minutes getting started on the index."

However, our negotiations may sometimes be impromptu, so learning to evaluate quickly what we want is essential.

Applying the Negotiating Litmus Test produces a *range* of possibilities, which enables you to keep sight of your own needs whilst allowing sufficient flexibility in your approach to produce a win-win outcome.

Ask yourself the five Negotiation Litmus questions.

1. "What do I want ideally?"
2. "What would I be happy with?"

3. "What would I be sufficiently satisfied with?"
4. "No, that's not enough, I also need . . ."
5. "This is now win-lose: I need to say no or withdraw."

Step 3 – Establish other peoples' needs and wants

What you need to do now is to establish others' needs and wants, rather than proclaim your own needs more stridently. We do this by asking questions.

Open questions

- Open questions are more helpful than closed questions in establishing real needs.
- Open questions open up areas of negotiation.
- Open questions handle objections or hassles.

Some of the most useful open questions start with:

"What . . .?"
"How . . .?"
"Why . . .?"
"When . . .?"
"Where . . .?"
"Who . . .?"

And phrases such as

"Tell me about . . .?"

Closed questions

Closed questions – are helpful in establishing clarification and agreement. They are particularly useful, in the context of the *verbal handshake* mentioned below'.

Closed questions start with:

"Do . . .?"
"Is . . .?"

"Have/Has . . .?"
"Are . . .?"
"If . . .?"

Step 4 – Getting agreement to both sets of needs and wants

After establishing the real needs, you may find that there are few or no differences, and that it is easy to reach a mutually satisfactory result. At other times it may seem that one set of needs can only be met at the expense of the other.

First of all, you need to:

* check that you have understood the other party's real needs and indicate your acknowledgement of them; and
* gain acceptance from the other party to agree and acknowledge your needs.

We call this a "*verbal handshake.*" This is a pivotal moment in the negotiation as future discussion is predicated on the basis that both sets of needs have validity.

There is no point to negotiating further if this is not so, as you will be now working with an unspoken win-lose, lose-lose agenda.

Below are two examples of a verbal handshake:

* Brian, I appreciate that you are reluctant to provide your support to this idea because you believe we haven't considered all the options.
  (Pause)
  Do you accept we are running out of time and need to make a decision today?

Or

- Jenny, I understand you want to borrow the car because it will be so much more convenient for you and your friends. (Pause)
  Do you appreciate that it will cost me more money and will mean I will have to get up considerably earlier to go to work by public transport whilst you have the car?

Step 5 – Creating solutions
The following questions encourage the other party to participate in creating win-win possibilities:

- " John, there must be a way round this . . ."
- "Sally, how about this as an idea . . .?"
- "Graham, how do you think this might work?"
- "Ranjit, what could be an alternative?"
- "Brigitta, what ideas have you for . . .?"

When you have debated and discussed the options you can then apply the *negotiation litmus test* and calibrate the level of *win-win*.

What stops us achieving win-win more often?

So, if win-win is so wonderful why doesn't everybody adopt it all the time?

At a logical level, who wouldn't choose an approach that gets you the best result and has a long shelf life? *Prima facie* it seems a no-brainer. However, we are not logical animals, but are made up of emotions, competing needs and a high degree of self-concern.

A win-win approach takes thought, courage, determination, effort, consideration and persistence.

It is relatively easy to adopt a win-lose approach. It is true you may have to expend energy to maintain a level of aggression, but you don't have to think too hard or really engage with the other person and consider their needs.

You need only consider *your* needs and wants. You can dig your heels in, demand, coerce, shout, threaten, be uncooperative, refuse to listen and focus on what you want.

Equally, when engaging in a lose-win approach, it is easy to give in and chose the path of least resistance. At least we are spared the unpleasant emotions of having to stick up for ourselves or seemingly disappoint others – all that messy conflict avoided.

With lose-lose we can really ease our hurt at missing out by ensuring that the other person involved doesn't get all they want, and won't enjoy the fruits of victory.

We also have to maintain some level of self-dignity and rationalize to ourselves why the defeat wasn't a devastating one and why we allowed ourselves to be coerced, bullied and manipulated. But there will be payback, if not today, some other time when we will exact subtle and sublime revenge: "Yes, I'll go to that party with you but I'll also let you know at every opportunity I'm miserable, hate being here and would much rather be somewhere else. That way you won't enjoy it either. Rather than say 'no', or negotiate with you (which takes effort etc.), I'd rather be a martyr and suffer."

The difference between win-win and compromise

In some people's eyes, compromise is seen as the same thing as a win-win approach. Compromise certainly shares some of the same characteristics and yet is also different.

On the positive side, compromise may seem the simplest, easiest and fairest way to cut up a fixed "pie" where there seems to be no chance of creating a bigger one. At least, it seems, everyone is sharing what is available. The negotiation does result in both parties having some of their needs meet.

On the downside, compromise may mean that both parties feel they might give away too much.

Sometimes compromise is seen as an acceptable form of lose-lose and you can settle for less when a better solution is available. If you settle too quickly for compromise you can sell yourself short.

The basic win-win approach means that you consider not only what you want but also what the other persons wants. You raise the degree of concern for both your own and the other party's needs. As with compromise, you are concerned with what is fair but you consult with others to explore needs and consider all possible options.

This increases the likelihood of reaching a solution, which encompasses more of everyone's needs, securing greater commitment to making the solution stick.

Giving and taking, when we know we have been listened to and heard, feels very different to compromising immediately.

Win-win is a long-term approach – recognizing in one situation you might not get what you think is sufficient but, overall, things will balance out. This is well illustrated in the case of a consultant, who came on one of our courses. Jim was owed money by a customer who was genuinely strapped for cash and couldn't pay the invoice when it became (long) overdue. There was a "history" between Jim and the company who had always sought to play fair with Jim.

Jim's conversation roughly went like this:

"I understand at the moment you are stretched for cash and I want to help. Are you prepared to make payments to me by regular installments over the next six months?"

I spoke to Jim some time later and I understood it took some time to be paid in full. But, far from losing what he wanted, Jim built a long-term relationship with the customer and was highly recommended to similar companies by his late-paying client.

Exercise

You may find it beneficial to do a quick audit of situations where you want to achieve a better solution than you are getting at the moment.

Write down three situations where you negotiated a solution with someone where there was a conflict between the needs of both parties.

Now list them in order of difficulty, the most difficult being the one that was also the most stressful.

Your list may have included tackling your boss for a salary increase, or asking your partner to clean the bath after he or she has finished. If you rated asking for a salary increase as the most difficult and most stressful thing to do, this would be number one on your list. While the bath cleaning question is a touchy one, you may give it a stress rating of just five.

Have a look at each situation and decide which of the four approaches you ended up using to resolve it, e.g. win-win; win-lose etc.

Did the approach you used achieve what you wanted?

No win, no play

Win-win is a negotiation, but it would be foolishly idealistic to contend that everyone wants to negotiate fairly – for one reason or another the other party may want to play "I win, you lose" and sometimes people will engage in lose-lose – a case of cutting off your nose to spite your face.

In no win, no play, you exercise your right not to get involved in the negotiation because the other party is not concerned with your win or the issue is not negotiable.

No win, no play is the position you convey to another party, the default position that asserts you are interested in negotiating provided the other party is interested in a solution. In saying the word "no" you are demonstrating that you are prepared to withdraw rather than pursue a fruitless activity, or engage in game playing, manipulation or threat.

No win, no play is a very powerful position, particularly when we feel the other party "holds all the cards" and we are power-less. Choosing to withdraw in these situations is more likely to maintain our integrity and respect, and to boost our confidence to tackle the most difficult of situations – a massive "leg up" for most of us.

Below is a process for saying "no" assertively, whilst still leaving the door open for further negotiation. If you don't say "no" the other party won't have to negotiate a win with you. It is, therefore, often a staging point towards a win-win negotiation.

The "No" Sandwich: saying "no" assertively

1. Acknowledge/empathize with the request	Show genuine listening. (Does not signify agreement or disagreement.)
2. Say "no" and give the real reason	Test: If this were not true would I say "yes." Differentiate between can't and won't. When you experience "hassle" maintain the original reason and do not invent or introduce new reasons. Use their name whenever you can.
3. Say what you are prepared to do/this time/what needs to be done in the future/offer a win-win. (You can also clarify the nature of the need.)	(1) You may decide to agree this time. (2) However, you need to register your committed position for the future and future action.

Example

1. Acknowledge or empathize	*Victor, I understand you're running late and would appreciate a lift home.*
2. Say "no"	*No, I can't give you a lift today because I am also running late and heading in the opposite direction to you.*
3. What you *are* prepared to do	*Next time you need a lift please ask and if I'm heading straight home I will be happy to give you one.*

Saying " no" assertively works because you are:

1. listening and empathizing
2. being clear and honest with your reasons (not excuses)
3. leaving the door open for a future win-win.

Exercise – saying "no" assertively

There may be situations in the past where you had the right to say no and you didn't, or a situation that is coming up in the future where it is important for you to say no.

Saying no is difficult for most of and the more you practise the better you become. Use the three steps mentioned above and write down what you want to say.

"...

....

..............."

Remember, when you say "no" the other party does not automatically give in, so consider some possible hassles or rebuttals the other party might employ. Involve a friend, partner or colleague and have some practice.

Do not change your reason, you might reword it, but it is the constancy of the "no" plus your real reason that gets the other party to accept this is your position.

Summary

Assertion is an attitude and a state of mind that requires a willingness to be flexible, to see the other person's view point and be prepared to really listen to what others are saying.

Assertiveness affects all areas of life. Assertive people tend to have fewer conflicts in their dealings with others, which translates into much less stress in their lives.

The win-win approach is about changing the conflict, from adversarial attack and defence, to co-operation. It is a powerful shift of attitude that alters the whole course of communication.

It is not about having wins *over* people but creating synergy by having wins *with* people.

The benefits of a win-win approach include:

- An increase in productivity (inside and outside of work).
- Encouraging creativity in people, inviting them to be open and flexible.
- An increase in commitment to higher quality solutions.
- Focusing energy and attention on solving problems rather than fighting with each other.
- Better, more caring relationships with others.
- Building trust with individuals as we behave in a way that demonstrates our own integrity as well as theirs.

The more flexible you become, the more choices you have regarding how you relate to others, and the more opportunities you have to resolve conflicts.

For the win-win approach to become the behaviour of choice it is necessary to develop additional skills to the ones we currently have. We need to learn to step back from some of our current solutions to consider the needs or concerns driving each person to particular outcomes.

3
It's All in the Mind

A basic difference between assertion and other behaviours is how our words and behaviour can affect the rights of others.

Assertiveness is an attitude of mind, with an accompanying set of *beliefs* about yourself and the world around you.

We talked in Chapter 2 about win-win being the central theme to assertion. Exercising win-win is evidence to others that you "walk the talk" and recognize that you live in an interdependent world where give and take is both necessary and desirable. Your needs matter, just as the needs of other people matter.

In this chapter we consider the mindset, and a set of mind tools that will help to provide you with the thinking processes that align your behaviour to your thoughts.

We look at the beliefs that are necessary to behave confidently, and communicate clearly what you need and want, whilst acknowledging the needs of others.

We also focus on the mental processes subtly at work that can derail your assertive intentions. We will notice how our internal chattering plays such a significant part in the results we achieve, and develop ways to empower and enable our assertive behaviour

Beliefs inform much of the self-chatter, so it is a good place to begin to understand how it is all in the mind.

Beliefs

Believe and act as if it were impossible to fail
Charles F Kettering

Much of what we do, say and feel, and how we act, is based on our values and beliefs, in particular our beliefs about ourselves and other people.

Problems occur when we hold non-assertive or aggressive beliefs about ourselves and about other people.

If you have assertive beliefs, then assertive behaviour will follow. If you do not hold assertive beliefs, then you will have difficulty in sustaining assertiveness and achieving win-win results.

The importance of beliefs

We normally think of beliefs in terms of creeds, canons or doctrine. Many beliefs are.

In the most fundamental way a belief is a guiding principle, dictum, or view that provides meaning and direction in life. We hold beliefs at an emotional level. Beliefs are a conviction and acceptance that certain things are true or real without the necessary supporting evidence that they are.

Our beliefs become:

- Filters to our perception of the world; we see, hear and feel what we want to see, hear and feel.
- Enabling or limiting to our behaviour potential and growth.
- Invisible, manifesting themselves through the actions we take.
- Self-fulfilling – "argue for your limitations and you have them."

Enabling or limiting beliefs

Limiting beliefs, whether aggressive or non-assertive, limit our growth, keep us fearful, anxious and insecure.

Limiting beliefs are those which constrain us in some way. Just by believing them, we do not think, do or say the things that they inhibit.

They invite us to think we are not worthy of love, success and respect and leave us feeling powerless and ineffective.

Enabling beliefs help you grow and build your confidence and realize your potential. Holding them helps you believe you can make a positive difference and support you to live a happier, healthy and successful life.

Non-assertive beliefs are generally those that assume we are not equal to other people, and hence drive non-assertive or aggressive behaviour.

Aggressive beliefs are generally those that assume we are superior to other people, and hence drive aggressive behaviour.

Assertive beliefs suggest we are on the same level and are equals and deserve the same amount of respect and communication as the next person

Below are examples of beliefs. Tick those which you think are examples of Aggressive, Non-assertive or Assertive beliefs.

Beliefs	Aggressive	Non-assertive	Assertive
1 I am more clever and more powerful than other people	√		
2 People who do not put themselves first deserve what's coming to them	√		

(Continued)

Assertiveness

Beliefs	Aggressive	Non-assertive	Assertive
3 I do not need permission to take action			√
4 I don't deserve to be successful like other people		√	
5 I am equal to others with the same rights as them			√
6 Other people cannot be trusted to do what they say they will	√		
7 It's ok to disagree – agreement is not always possible or desirable			√
8 I will never change, this is the way I am	√	√	
9 You've got to be ruthless to get on in the world	√		
10 Others think I am weak if I ask for help	√	√	
11 I need to be stronger than others or I will be taken for granted	√		
12 You need to tread on a few toes to get what you want	√		
13 I am not responsible for others' actions, decisions or feelings			√
14 I'll get in trouble if I express my feelings		√	

Where do our beliefs come from?

Many of our beliefs are formed at an early age – the Jesuits used to have a saying, *"Give me the child until he's seven, and I will show you the man."*

1. **Our childhood.** Sadly, the "child' within us may form false and limiting conclusions as a result of being told, "You're just showing off, you just want attention!" and may find it hard in later life to speak positively about their achievements and strengths, or to accept praise graciously.

2. **Important people.** We may have picked up sayings, dictums and prejudices from "important" people in our lives. These can be parents, grandparents, teachers or significant others. We love or respect them and learn to trust what they say without reservation.

    Many a child's educational talent has been blighted because they have been told by a teacher they are not good at maths, art, science or whatever, and believe this to be true. Contrast this with the teacher who inspires and gives you every belief that you are special, talented or gifted.

3. **Social or cultural.** We are influenced by the social and cultural values which reward certain behaviours and punish others. The company we work for may embody a particular view about customers or clients, or ways of treating staff. We've both lived and worked for a number of years in parts of the world where the culture dictates that seniority is the most influential status. We never challenged the elder even if we knew they were wrong. We had to find other ways to change things.

4. **Traumatic events.** We may experience traumatic events that throw us into a state of shock. From this state we frequently draw conclusions, which may be helpful or unhelpful.

    A friend had a bad road accident whilst sitting in the passenger seat of the car. To this day she has an unshaken belief that the passenger seat is the most dangerous seat in the car and will only sit in the back behind the driver.

5. **Excuses.** One reason we use faulty logic and form limiting beliefs is to excuse ourselves from what we perceive to be our failures.

When we do something and it does not work, we often explain away our failure by forming and using beliefs which justify our actions and leave us blameless. Until recently Conrad has never been able to repair anything significant that goes wrong in our house. His previous attempts invariably meant paying a handyman to repair the bigger mess he made. His excuse: "I've never been practically minded."

6. **Fear.** Limiting beliefs are often driven by fear. Locking the belief in place is the fear that, if we go against the beliefs, our fundamental needs will be harmed.

There is often a strong social component to our decisions and the thought of criticism, ridicule or rejection by others is enough to powerfully inhibit us. We also fear that we may be harmed in some way by others, and so avoid them or seek to appease them.

12 steps to developing an assertive belief

Holding an assertive belief is the first step towards behaving with confidence.

Beware of thinking that by having an assertive belief you can sit back and let things happen – it needs to be developed and supported by action.

There are 12 steps to developing and stabilizing assertive beliefs that will help you to become more assertive.

Steps

1. Analyze the situations where you are not achieving the results you want.
2. Identify whether there are any limiting beliefs that are holding you back – write them down – to write something means you now have some control over it.
3. Challenge these beliefs from the adult, less emotional, part of your brain.
4. Identify the origin of these limiting beliefs, what happened long ago to cause you to believe this? It helps to put things into perspective.
5. What is the benefit of holding this belief? Any behaviour we repeat has a benefit. For instance, when we don't stand up for ourselves we may not get what we want but, initially, it does give us a sense of relief and release of tension.
6. What is the assertive belief you now want to hold? Write it down or represent it visually – it helps focus the mind. Pin it to the wall. Carry it with you in your bag or pocket.
7. What is the benefit for you and others if you hold this belief?
8. What permission to do certain things do you need to give yourself and others? (See the Rights section below.)
9. What do you need to tell yourself? (See the Self-Talk section later in this chapter.)
10. Start by acting assertively. You may not feel it, but you can always behave as if you do.
11. Start small: be assertive in relatively simple contexts, such as asking for things in shops and restaurants where it is not a "life or death" situation.
12. Reflect on your successes. Realize how the new belief is making a difference.

Rights

You are free to choose but you are not free from the consequences of your choice.

Anon

When we are unsure of ourselves, or uncertain about the situation, we may not assert ourselves.

"I am not really comfortable in some situations and find it difficult to confront my true feelings. I want to say what I really want, but I feel inhibited and I don't think I have the right – in case I say something I may regret or feel guilty about.

"I have a need for other people's approval and I fear rejection, so I remain submissive and then feel bad for not sticking up for myself when I think I have the right."

These are the words of Judith, a respected and competent senior manager. Judith behaves assertively in most situations but, when working with colleagues in meetings, clams up, withdraws and contributes little to the discussions and decisions.

Judith could look at her limiting beliefs in this and similar situations, but could also make some more immediate changes in her behaviour if she considers her *rights* – the rights she is denying herself and others.

Assertiveness is an open and honest expression of your feelings, opinions and needs, and a way of communicating what you want clearly, respecting your own rights and those of others.

Rights is an issue of personal permission, the inner voice that says it is justified and OK to do or say something.

Each of us is born with unique potential and free will to:

- decide for ourselves,
- make mistakes and learn from them,

- refuse requests,
- say "no" without feeling guilty,
- be ourselves,
- say I don't know, and
- refuse to have to make a decision NOW.

An important step in becoming assertive is to become aware of our rights as an individual, and to reaffirm some of the basic rights which verify our uniqueness, identity and personal power.

Clarifying our rights is more than an intellectual stock take. At an intellectual level, most people would agree that they have the rights described below. However, unless you enact the rights you do not have them.

If you have recurring situations where you are not getting the desired results, it could be that you are being unclear about your rights in those situations, or have not made them come true by your actions, or have acted in a way that removed the rights of others.

Below are some general rights that apply in a range of situations. It's important to know what rights you currently accept for yourself and act upon, and what rights you give to others and allow them to act upon. From here, you can decide what further rights you need to operate with in order to strengthen your assertion.

Exercise

From the list below, evaluate each right you give yourself and others by marking a score between 1 and 10.

A score of 1 would be, "I hardly ever give myself this right."

A score of 10 would mean, "I always give myself this right."

A score of 5 would be, "I sometimes give myself this right."

(*Continued*)

Tick the ones I give myself	Bill of Rights	Tick the ones I give others
	I have the right to say "yes" and "no" without feeling guilty or selfish	
	I have the right to have my own opinions and ideas (and have these heard)	
	I have the right to have needs (that may be different from others' needs)	
	I have the right to ask that others respond to my needs and wants	
	I have the right to be human e.g. to make a mistake or say "I don't know"	
	I have the right to change my mind, and to "change"	
	I have the right to have feelings and to express them assertively	
	I have the right to be "me" (to be different from others, or what they want me to be, or do)	
	I have the right to make my own decisions and to deal with the consequences	
	I have the right to have others respect my rights	
	I have the right to be treated with respect and dignity	

Tick the ones I give myself	Bill of Rights	Tick the ones I give others
	I have the right to be listened to and be taken seriously	
	I have the right to judge my own behaviour, thoughts and emotions, and to be responsible for the consequences	
	I have the right to say I don't understand	
	I have the right to ask for what I want (realizing that the other person has the right to say "no")	

Although the values you have given are subjective they will have importance to you.

When you have completed the exercise:

* Contrast your scores on the left (you give to yourself) with those on the right (you give to others). Are the scores the same?
* Higher scores on the right rather than on the right indicate in your view you may behave aggressively in certain situations.
* Conversely, higher scores on the right may indicate that you behave non-assertively or submissively in certain situations.
* Where is your lowest score? Would enacting that right get you better results in certain situations and with certain people?

Identify those situations where you would like to act assertively and write down the rights you need to act on for yourself and the rights you need to maintain for the other person.

Much is talked of rights these days. Every right you claim has an equal responsibility associated with it.

I believe I have the right to make a mistake. I also have the right to:

(a) take responsibility, acknowledge the mistake openly and honestly;
(b) learn from it and rectify it;
(c) not make the same mistake again; and
(d) ask for help if necessary.

Exercise – Determining your rights

In the following six situations decide what rights you have and what rights the other person has.

1. A close relative of your partner, with whom you prefer not to spend much time, rings up. She says that she is planning to spend the next three weeks with you.
   YOUR RIGHTS   THEIR RIGHTS

2. One of your children has come home later than the agreed time for the last two days.
   YOUR RIGHTS   THEIR RIGHTS

3. You are enjoying a meal at a restaurant and someone starts talking very loudly at a table close by, which you find disturbing.
   YOUR RIGHTS   THEIR RIGHTS

4. You arrive home from work and your partner wants to go to the movies, but you would rather not.
   YOUR RIGHTS   THEIR RIGHTS

5. You have made a mistake in preparing a report for your boss. Your boss starts telling you off in front of the rest of your colleagues.
YOUR RIGHTS   THEIR RIGHTS

6. It is your turn to do the dishes. Before you get up from the table, your partner begins to tell you that the last time you did the dishes they had to do them again and the kitchen was a mess when you'd finished.
YOUR RIGHTS   THEIR RIGHTS

Devil or angel – self-talk

Everyone has an evil twin

Anon

Sometimes, it is as though we hear the voices of two little people perched on our shoulder: the devil and the angel.

The angel supports you with positive thoughts emphasizing what you *can* do, and whispering calm, confident thoughts about possibility and potential:

"You can do this, it may be a stretch, you've done similar things before, you have succeeded in the past, with thought and commitment you can do so again . . ."

It is the creative, empowering part of you, inviting you to think beyond your frailties and concentrate on your capabilities and strengths.

Its purpose is to protect you, keep you safe and nurture your development.

The devil, the other voice, is full of self-doubt and admonition:

"You can't do that, you'd be foolish to try, look what happened last time, told you you'd be no good at it, you're not clever enough, you're not good enough, take the easy option . . ." It preys on your failings and fears and prohibits you from taking risks.

This voice hustles for control, drowning out the angel in you and emphasizing what can go wrong, what you can't do. It plays on your anxieties.

Perversely, although the purpose of this nagging voice is also to protect you and keep you safe from harm, it chooses a destructive and negative way to achieve this positive intention.

Have you ever experienced that? Which one wins?

Donoma's story

There is an old North American Indian tale about a revered chief, Donoma. Every night, he would gather the young braves together to educate them about their heritage, and the path of the Indian brave.

"Sometimes," he said, "there will be a part of you that wants to do well and you will be full of your own strength and wisdom – you will be in the grip of the white bear for he is strong and is good.

"And other times you will doubt yourself, be fearful and will want to give up – for you are in the hold of the brown bear and he is strong as well.

"And through all the suns and moons of your life, the white and brown bear will be with you. Both seek to be in control, both are at each other's throats, fighting to the death.

"Sometimes the brown bear will be stronger and you will bend to his will and, other times, the white bear will be in control and you will follow his path. And they will fight with each constantly.

One moment the white bear is on top, and is the stronger of the two, driving the brown bear down into submission.

Other times the brown bear is in the ascendancy, forcing the white bear to submit and yield. And the struggle goes on."

One of the braves stood up with a confused and quizzical look and asked, "which bear is stronger and which one wins in the end?"

The old chief drew himself up to his full height. After a lengthy pause he said, "It is hard to tell my son because it all depends on which one you feed."

Eliminate the emotions and then be successful

When you can manage your emotions, you can immediately become more assertive.

However, our emotions are a product of how we think about ourselves, others or any other factors in any situation.

Almost always, once you eliminate any anger, fear, stress, anxiety or any other powerful negative emotion, you automatically become more empowered and capable of dealing with any problem or difficulty.

We talk to ourselves more than anyone else

We talk to ourselves more than anyone else during our day. Before we do something, we rehearse what we are going to say and how we are going to say it. Whilst we are in the heat of battle we are chattering away to ourselves and, as we walk away, we are analyzing what we did, and could or should have said. This self-chatter is constant.

Sometimes we talk ourselves into things and sometimes we talk ourselves out of things. Sometimes we talk ourselves up but, most of the time, we talk ourselves down. These are the two twins, the devil or angel, the white bear or brown bear.

A fundamental model of human behaviour asserts that these internal conversations have a direct impact on our behaviour.

If we are influenced by what others say to us and about us, how much more are we influenced by what we say to ourselves?

The devil or angel chatter helps determine how we *feel*, which in turn shapes how we *act*. This *internal conversation* can consist of verbal exchanges inside our head and, at other times, can be pictures or a movie that we run inside our head.

Much of the time we are not conscious of what we are saying to ourselves, the chatter happens in an instant, at a level below our conscious awareness.

We may not always be aware of those thoughts, but we do become aware of unpleasant feelings and end up behaving in an aggressive or non-assertive way.

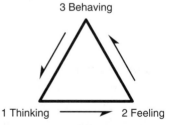

Think–Feel–Act model of behaviour (1)

When we have "faulty," (i.e. aggressive or non-assertive) thoughts, this leads to unproductive feelings such as anxiety, fear, anger, resentment, helplessness, etc. This can result in us behaving angrily, accusingly, anxiously, submissively, and so on.

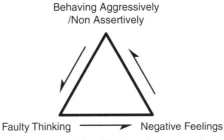

Think–Feel–Act model of behaviour: Faulty Thinking

Such an internal process will guarantee that we will not be at our best, making it difficult to achieve win-win outcomes.

Conversely, when our thinking is positive and realistic, we feel confident, satisfied, receptive, interested, calm, etc. This leads us to be creative, resilient, able to cope, optimistic and realistic.

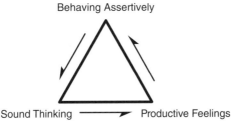

Think–Feel–Act model of behaviour: Sound Thinking

Just imagine relaxing at home, in a comfortable chair, watching a TV programme that you've been wanting to see for weeks, or listening to a favourite piece of music, with a glass of wine or some other beverage to your liking. All is well with the world.

The tranquility is shattered by the door bursting open. A neighbour enters with a large dustbin, and empties it in front of you. All is now not well with the world. There in front of you is a pile of rotting, evil-smelling garbage that infects the very air that you breathe. What do you do?

1. Invite him in and ask him when his next delivery is?
2. Invite him in and have a cosy chat about his wife, children and where he is going on his next holiday?
3. Threaten him verbally and physically?
4. Ask him to remove the waste, compensate you for a ruined carpet, and request that he never does this again?
5. Continue "relaxing" as if nothing has happened?

You have a choice

When the results you are getting are not what you want, you are not simply destined to repeat history. You can intervene at the *thinking* stage or the *feeling* stage and thus change what you do and, therefore, the result.

We may not always be responsible for the situations we get ourselves into but we are responsible for our behaviour within those situations. We have choice.

Once we know our behaviour is predicated on this simple model we can decide:

- how we want to be in a future situation, and
- how we want to be in the situation as it's happening.

The first thing you need to do to regain control is to bring the negative thoughts to your conscious attention.

You need to slow down your thinking and look at, or listen to, what you are seeing in your mind's eye or saying to yourself.

Step 1
Ask: *what am I saying to myself?* Or, if your thoughts are represented with a picture or video: *what am I seeing?*

Step 2
Listen to the answer. Many people find it helpful to write down what they are thinking or describe what they are seeing.

As you start to learn to use this "tool" I'd recommend you write down your thoughts, as it allows you to challenge them dispassionately.

Step 3
Challenge the bits of your thinking you believe are not helpful in supporting your success, i.e. thinking that is faulty.

Characteristics of faulty thinking
Below are some characteristics of faulty thinking:

- **Pessimistic prediction of the future.** They are only interested in themselves and no one will be interested in what I have to say.
- **Absolute thinking.** You've let me down before so I can't rely on you again.
- **Exaggerating.** Everybody says that everything that could possibly go wrong will go wrong and I know everyone agrees with that.
- **Assumptions.** It's going to be very hard for me to become more assertive.
- **Mind reading.** When they stare at me I know they're thinking I don't know what I'm talking about.
- **Unbalanced view.** The last time I spoke I got everything back to front, I'm sure they didn't understand a thing.
- **Negative focus.** I won't ever be able to ask for what I want.

Step 4

Convert your faulty thinking into positive and realistic thoughts. Produce a script that is made up of entirely sound and balanced thoughts.

Characteristics of positive self-talk

Below are some characteristics of positive self-talk:

- **Realistic view of the future.** It may not be easy for me, but I have prepared well and I can trust my intuition to get me through.
- **Objective.** They have a right to question me and challenge how far we've progressed with the programme. I can be honest and give them my view.
- **Noticing the positive.** I know information that senior people don't, that's why they've have asked me to attend this meeting.
- **Honest about the past.** They have listened in the past and I can explain how the concerns of the staff are affecting the programme.
- **Can-do approach.** I can trust myself to say the right thing, I can be firm and direct with Giles and stay committed to what I believe.

Worst-case scenarios

Our darkest and deepest fears are sometimes well camouflaged and unexpressed, except as profound, unhealthy feelings of unease and dread. Not all fears are equal. We tend to exaggerate certain fears. When not challenged they become the most potent disabler of our potential. The worst-case scenario may happen but, by bringing it to our conscious attention, we have control and can plan what we can do about it should it occur.

Challenge yourself to answer these questions as logically as you can. Could that really happen? How likely is it? What can I do?

This kind of thinking liberates us from the tyranny of the unknown. Most of the time you will realize that the likelihood of the worst-case scenario happening is minimal. Go on, try it. What's the worst that can happen?

When you are being successful and achieving win-win outcomes you are clearly doing a lot right and, unless you run into storms along the way, you may not need realistic thinking techniques: "if it ain't broke, don't fix it."

For those times, however, when you feel

* under pressure
* threatened
* lacking your normal self-confidence

or you think you're facing disaster and it is not going to work out well for you, then it's time to reach out for some extra help.

Remember that faulty thinking is the first stage in developing unhealthy and negative feelings that drive behaviour and give you results you don't want. Faulty thinking is often a rehearsal for failure and is self-fulfilling!

Sound thinking produces an entirely different set of feelings and emotions that enable us to be at our best. It is a rehearsal for success and is also self-fulfilling!

Below are four situations to practice changing faulty thinking. The first three are example scenarios and the fourth gives you an opportunity to take a situation of your own and apply the process to your own scenario.

Convert any faulty self-talk in the left-hand column to positive thinking in the right-hand column.

Situation 1

Alex is thinking about his job interview tomorrow. He's had a few interviews but received no feedback about how he did. Here are a few of his thoughts.

Faulty self-talk	Positive self-talk
"I can prepare all I want but it doesn't seem to get me anywhere"	"If I plan I'll be ready for most things they'll ask me and have a better chance of being calm and collected"
"I won't be able to answer their questions"	"I can stay calm, breathe slowly and take my time – I usually know the answers"
"They are probably looking for someone more dynamic than me"	"There probably isn't a perfect match but I fit what they have asked for or they would not have asked me to interview. I believe I can do the job very well"
"I'll make a fool of myself if I'm not careful"	"I can only give it my best shot and then it's up to them"
⇩	⇩

Negative feelings	Productive Feelings

Fear	Calm
Anxiety	Focused
Worry	Reassured
Nervous and anxious	Quietly confident

Behaviour	Behaviour

Hesitant and unsure	Attentive
Indecisive	Open
Reluctant	Interested
Resigned	Interesting
Sceptical	Relaxed
	Self-assured

Situation 2

Your partner has been easily provoked into an argument the last few times you've disagreed with him/her. He or she has volunteered you to help out in a local fete and it clashes with something else you want to do.

Consider what positive self-talk you might use in this situation.

Self-talk	Positive self-talk

I don't want yet another argument – why can't we discuss things rationally?	It doesn't have to be an argument, we talk about most things rationally
I'll have to be very forceful to get him/her to listen	I know I can stay calm and say things on an even keel
S/he will become defensive	She or he may become defensive but I can listen, let him/her finish what they have to say
I'll lose my cool and we'll be at each other's throats	
But I'm not going to stand for it anymore, I'll give as good as I get	I can confidently say how I feel rather than blame them for my feelings
	If it becomes personal I can pause and take my time and focus on what I want

Negative feelings	Productive Feelings
Taken for granted	Assured
Put down	At ease
Over ruled	Balanced
Resentful	Calm
Angry	Capable
Wary	Composed
Tired	Courageous

(Continued)

Behaviour	Behaviour
Walking on eggshells	Listening to different perspectives and different views
Picking up on emotive words	
Lack of eye contact	Understanding others' needs and establishing what is important about you being volunteered
Rising aggression	
Poor listening	Acknowledging, not necessarily agreeing with emotions
Another row in the making, or walking away feeling defeated	Good eye contact
	Questions
	Staying firm and connected to the discussion
	Building a pattern of discussion that is different from arguing

Situation 3

Lately, when you are out in a social gathering, one of your friends has routinely made fun of you and put you down. You suspect it will happen again when you go out with them this evening.

Consider what positive self-talk you might use in this situation.

Self-talk	Positive self-talk

Here we go again I can see it now, I'll be embarrassed and feel so small

I'll have to just sit there and take whatever they say

I'll have to avoid all contact with him/her

If I make a comment she/he will raise her eyebrows and roll their eyes

If I say anything to him/her they will just laugh it off, tell me to grow up and not take everything personally

I can see myself open and looking firm

I can breathe slowly and deeply and stay in control of my feelings

I can acknowledge what they say and, if they put me down, ask questions such as, "What makes you say that?"

I can hold on to my integrity and also maintain the integrity of the other person

I can pull them to one side and ask what they are getting from the put-downs

I can explain the effect it has on my feelings and our friendship

I can listen calmly to their replies

I can say that I'd like our relationship to be on the basis of mutual trust

(Continued)

Negative feelings	Productive Feelings

Cut down   Composed

Insulted   Constant

Embarrassed   Centred

Mocked   Expressive

Ridiculed   Friendly

Teased   Genuine

                     Honest

Behaviour	Behaviour
Tense and taught	Relaxed
Edgy	Upright, still posture
False smiles	Relaxed facial expression
Looking inward	Direct eye contact
Speaking faster	Questioning their derogatory comments
Less confident in what you say, apologizing and hedging	with "what makes you say/think that?"
	Moderate pace and volume
Looking uncomfortable and wanting be somewhere else	Open gestures
	Staying put
Leaving early, feeling resentful	

Situation 4

Choose a difficult situation you have to face in the future, one where you have bad or negative feelings about a situation or someone.

As you think about it, write down what you are thinking NOW. Write down all your thoughts in the left-hand column.

Challenge your thinking in the left-hand column and change any faulty thinking to the right-hand column. How would you feel now? How do you think you will handle the situation when it does occur?

Faulty self-talk	Positive self-talk
⬇	⬇
Negative feelings	Productive feelings
⬇	⬇
Behaviour	Behaviour

When the situation is going wrong – in real time

So far we have been concentrating on conversations and situations that have not yet occurred. How you prepare your mindset, prior to a situation, will play a significant part in the result you get.

The self-talk techniques work equally well during a conversation or situation that may not be going well for you. The usual telltale signs of feelings and emotions will flag up discomfort and unease.

The more you use the self-talk techniques, the quicker you become adept at changing your state of mind to how you want it to be.

In any situation we are not talking all the time. When you take a pause, or use a moment of silence, you can ask yourself, "what am I saying to myself?" The reply is swift, you can become skilled at challenging your thinking and substituting faulty thinking for sound.

Is this just kidology?

Can you really change the outcome of a situation by changing the words inside your head? Is it enough just to affirm sound thoughts or, in reality, would you just be kidding yourself?

Just saying the words may help, and it certainly is an important first step. On its own, however, it is unlikely to make the difference unless accompanied by belief, effort and assertive action. Motivation also plays a huge part: how much do you really want to do behave this way and what is the reward?

"But what," I hear you say, "if I say the words and still I don't have the feelings associated with them? Am I like Frazer in *Dad's Army*, "doomed?"

The answer, of course, is "no" – there are other mental resources you can tap into.

Back to the future

We were enthralled and frightened by the original film, *Jaws* – the story of a gigantic white shark that terrifies the small island community of Amity. The image of the shark fin cutting through the water, the sound of the pulsating, rhythmic pounding of the music building to a frenetic crescendo, and the flailing feet of the swimmers . . .

We found the music haunting and dramatic and, whenever we hear it, we're transported back to those images and sounds and we experience the moment all over again.

It's not only *Jaws*. There is lots of music that evokes special memories and feelings, and not all of them good. We imagine that is why the nostalgic replay of "golden oldies" on the radio is so successful.

We have the same experience with smells. Some of us were always terrified of going to the dentist and there was a particular dental anaesthetic smell and perhaps even the smell of the rubber mask that was put over you to deliver "gas." Whenever you come across any of those smells you may find yourself shivering, your mood changes, the hairs on the back of your neck stand up, your heart pounds and you break into a sweat.

Pleasant or unpleasant, both our body and our mind remember and store that memory for future retrieval. Useful for us because, even if at the present time we do not feel vibrant and confident, providing we can find a quiet moment to think about it we can access these feelings via memory. We can bring the feelings into the present and let them work in service for our own good. What you need to do is to go back to a time when you were, for instance, feeling successful, in good humour, brimming with confidence, and picture yourself there, hear yourself there, and feel what you felt as you experienced these states of being.

Ah, you might say, BUT what if I have never felt those emotions, or they were such a long time ago, that I can't retrieve them from my dim and distant past?

So, here's a further good bit of news for you.

It seems your clever brain cannot distinguish imagination from reality.

You can ask a different question of your brain, "If I did feel confident/vibrant/convincing . . . What would it feel like? You can take these feelings back into your present as if they were real to you.

Feelings exercise

Expressing yourself clearly and dispassionately will help develop and maintain healthy relationships both professionally and personally.

One of the many interesting things we've noticed on our courses is the limited vocabulary that people use to express their feelings. Being able to name the feeling is useful in getting touch with it, and becoming more authentic in your communication. Articulating your emotions is one way of clarifying them. Hearing the words spoken helps reinforce what is being felt.

You might like to explore your ability to "retrieve" emotions from past memories by using these feeling words – you could also try words that you think you haven't felt for a while or have never felt before and imagine what they would feel like.

accepted	accomplished	adaptable	admirable
adored	ambitious	appreciated	assured
at ease	attentive	attractive	authentic
balanced	beautiful	blessed	brave
bright	brilliant	calm	capable
centred	certain	cheerful	cherished
clear	complete	confident	courageous
decisive	delighted	dependable	distinguished
dynamic	ecstatic	efficient	elated
elegant	empowered	energized	enthusiastic
excited	expressive	flexible	focussed
forceful	Friendly	Fulfilled	gifted
graceful	grounded	happy	helpful
heroic	honest	hopeful	humorous
in control	independent	influential	inspired
intelligent	invincible	joyful	jubilant
kind	liberated	loved	lucky
			(*Continued*)

masterful	mindful	methodical	motivated
noble	non judgemental	open hearted	
organized	outgoing	passionate	patient
peaceful	perfect	pleasant	positive
powerful	prepared	present	quick
rational	reassured	receptive	relaxed
resolute	respected	secure	self-reliant
sensational	sensitive	skilful	steadfast
tenacious	tender	thoughtful	tolerant
unbiased	understood	unique	valued
vital	warm	wise	worthwhile

Is it a weakness to talk about feelings? The answer is "no" according to mental health research. Talking about feelings productively strengthens you, both physically and emotionally.

Before you can talk about your feelings you need to be able to name them.

We hope the exercise has helped you extend your "feelings" vocabulary words so that you can be more specific about them and help someone else understand how you are really feeling.

Being able to be specific about feelings is helpful not only in general conversation but is particularly useful when later in this book we look at "assertive options" and "negative feelings assertion."

Finally, take full responsibility for your feelings rather than blame others. Nobody makes you feel anything: loved, angry, depressed, elated and so on – it is a choice YOU make.

Summary

Creation occurs twice, firstly in your mind as you think through and design what you are going to say and, secondly, in the reality you create.

Beliefs are deep, unconsciously held master programmes that determine our more specific thoughts and action. Beliefs act like the operating system on your computer allowing you to select programmes to achieve specific results.

Beliefs, often programmed in at an early age, either act as empowering or disempowering influences. You need to identify and challenge those beliefs that are disempowering, replacing them with beliefs that empower, develop and grow your assertive skills.

Closer to your level of conscious control are the conversations you have with yourself, the inner dialogues that are a product of your beliefs. These have an immediate effect on the way you behave. Those internal conversations that emanate from disempowering beliefs tend to generate faulty thinking, which then leads to unproductive feelings and behaviour that does us no favours, to put it mildly.

Fortunately you have the means to change these thoughts by challenging them and substituting more realistic positive thinking. Your realistic and positive thinking creates productive feelings inside that lead to assertive behaviour.

You now have the mental tools to carry in to your actual conversations with people. Not only are first impressions important with a new relationship but the beginnings of conversations are instrumental in setting up the atmosphere and mood.

If you feel confident and open, this will be the impression you give before you have even spoken a word. If you feel nervous, anxious or suspicious your body will communicate this to the person you are speaking to.

Exactly what you do to outwardly represent your inner life – in the words you use and the impression you give – are covered in the next chapter when we develop assertive communication tools.

4
Assertive Communication

The ability to communicate effectively has implications for every part of life. Assertive communication can improve family relationships, enhance business relationships and improve the quality of life.

Assertive communication is your ability to transmit a message to someone else in a way that faithfully replicates it in someone else's mind, i.e. they clearly understand. Equally, assertive communication is your ability to receive someone else's message in a similar way, i.e. you understand.

The effectiveness of your communication is measured by the response you get. In other words *you* are responsible for the communication. If the response is different to what you expected it is likely you have created a disparity between the words and the music. The good news is this: It's in your sphere of control and you can change it.

In this chapter we look at the reasons why effective communication is hijacked by transmitting different messages with words and body language, and what to do to make it effective.

We'll look at the words you use and how you say them to determine whether your communication will be interpreted as being non-assertive, aggressive or assertive.

We'll see how the non-verbal elements of your message play a significant part in clarity and understanding. These elements particularly apply to face-to-face interaction, but also affect other forms of remote communication such as the telephone and the written word.

The aim in effective communication is not only to transmit information, but also emotions and feelings to create enduring relationships. You cannot guarantee others will want to understand everything you say from an altruistic viewpoint – communication works best when it is two-way.

For your communication to be effective, and the relationship to work, you need to show interest in other peoples' ideas and, more importantly, you need to show interest in them.

You need to create the conditions where mutuality is sustainable by establishing rapport. We will demonstrate a number of ways to create and maintain rapport. We are convinced from our experience of working with people that the most significant and potent way to do this is through assertive listening.

Finally, we'll introduce you to a number of assertive options to use to maintain your assertion in everyday interactions, and in those more trying and difficult situations where you require a range of assertive communication tools to bring about win-win.

The danger of mixed messages

Joanna found her husband's habit of interrupting her and finishing off her sentences increasingly annoying. Today she resolved she was going to talk to him about it. Joanna tended to avoid any kind of conflict and wanted to do this with a "light" touch without hurting Tim's feelings.

Joanna felt proud of herself after she had spoken to Tim, and looked forward to the change in their relationship. However, days went by and she became more deflated as nothing had seemed to change.

Plucking up the courage again she reminded Tim he had agreed to stop interrupting her but was now doing it as frequently as ever.

"I thought you agreed," she said, "that you would try from now on not to interrupt me like you did before but you are doing it as much as you were before."

"I didn't think you were serious about it," Tim laughed, "because you were smiling and joking when you said it. How was I to know you meant it?"

Have you ever said anything to somebody that was misinterpreted or misunderstood? When someone says "I love you," how do you really know whether they mean it? If you don't get the response you had hoped for, chances are that you have been hijacked by one of the golden rules of communication: *make what you say and how you say it be congruent.* Your non-verbal behaviour needs to be in tune with your words – you need the words to match the music.

Two levels of communication

We communicate on at least two different levels:

- at the level of content – *what* you say, and
- at the level of emotions – the *way* you say it.

In the 1960s, Professor Albert Mehrabian and colleagues at the University of California conducted research into human communication patterns. This involved spoken communication and is particularly useful in illustrating the importance of factors other than words when trying to convey or interpret meaning in a communication. Such elements included posture, distance/space, gestures, facial expressions, head movement, eye contact; and the non-verbal aspects of speech such as tone, volume, speed, emphasis, pauses and speech itself.

Mehrabian's research has provided the basis for these oft-quoted statistics for the effectiveness of spoken communication:

- 7% of the message pertaining to feelings and attitudes is in the words that are spoken.
- 38% of the message is attributable to feelings and attitudes in the voice.
- 55% of the message is attributable to feelings and attitudes in facial expression, posture and gestures.

Care, however, needs to be taken not to generalize these findings into all forms of communication scenarios. The value of Mehrabian's theory relates to communications where the emotional content in the meaning of the message is significant and the need to understand it is great.

Mehrabian's research

In the first study, "subjects" were asked to listen to a recording of a woman's voice saying the word "maybe" in three different ways to convey liking, neutrality and disliking. They were also shown photos of the woman's face conveying the same three emotions. Following this, the subjects were then asked to guess the emotions:

- heard in the recorded voice,
- seen in the photos, and
- from both the voice and photos together.

The result? The subjects correctly identified the emotions 50% more often from the photos in scenario 2 than from the voice alone.

In the second study, subjects were asked to listen to nine recorded words:

- "Honey," "dear," "thanks" (words meant to convey liking).
- "Maybe," "really," "oh" (words to convey neutrality).
- "Don't," "brute," "terrible" (words to convey disliking).

Each word was pronounced in three different ways and the subjects were asked to guess the emotions being conveyed. The results suggested that the subjects were more influenced by the tone of voice than by the words themselves.

It was the combined statistical results of these two studies that led Professor Mehrabian to come up with the now widely quoted and much over simplified statistic rule:

Communication is 7% verbal and 93% non-verbal

Professor Mehrabian's conclusion was that, for inconsistent or contradictory communications, body language and tonality may be more accurate indicators of meaning and emotions than the words alone.

How to spot the body language associated with aggression, non-assertion and assertion

It would be misleading to extrapolate Mehrabian's conclusions to all types of communication, as his formula was established in situations where there was an incongruence between the words and the expression.

What is clear, however, is that you need to make the words and elements of body language congruent with each other. This will aid impact, influence and *understanding*.

Where there is a conflict between the words and the music, we tend to put more credence in the music.

If you are thinking and planning what you are going to say, you can think long and hard about the words you use. These are a product of your conscious thought.

Our non-verbal behaviour on the other hand is not as controllable as it is a product of our feelings and attitudes which are more the domain of our unconscious mind. What we are not conscious of, by definition, we cannot control. If you are a masterful actor you may be able to fool others and disguise these intrusive emotions, but for the rest of us in everyday interactions there isn't the time or the skill to fake it.

The implications for this are endless. So, in future, when you are listening to someone, pay as much attention to the music as to the words. If there is a mismatch all may not seem as it appears! The next time you ask someone to do something for you and they say "yes" pay attention to the non-verbal elements or you may be dealing with the counterfeit "no" or a "perhaps" when what you thought you heard was a definite "yes."

Similarly, when you speak, remember your body is talking as much as your mouth is.

We can recognize aggression, non-assertion and assertion, both from the actual words, the language, and the non-verbal behaviour we use.

Example characteristics of body language associated with the three styles (*note that a single element of body language is not enough to indicate the behaviour, you need to observe a cluster of behaviours*)

	Aggressive	Non-assertive	Assertive
Posture	An overall tightening of the body, becoming more rigid and static	Collapsed, inward nervous movements, shrugs and shuffles	Open and relaxed, sit/stand with feet placed firmly on the floor and head held up (earthed)
			Centred, relaxed

	Aggressive	Non-assertive	Assertive
The voice	Very firm, tone is sarcastic, sometimes cold and clinical, hard and sharp, strident, often shouting, and usually rising at the end	Sometimes shaky, over soft and apologetic, often dull and monotone, quiet and drops away at the end of the sentence, mumbling, hesitant	Steady and firm, appropriate to the context, sincere and clear, tone middle range with warmth and emphasis, not over loud or quiet – middle range
The face	Disapproving frowns, pursed lips, sneers or full snarls, scowls, eyebrows raised in amazement or disbelief, rolling of the eyes, anger signs such as redness of the face, jaw set firm, chin thrust forward	False smile masking other emotions, collapsing inwards	Open and free from tension, smiles when pleased, frowns when angry, facial expression is congruent with the message, jaw relaxed
Eyes	Used to stare and hold the gaze for long periods, staring and dominating or not bothering to make any eye contact, looking away and being dismissive	Minimal or no eye contact, looking away, looking down, averting the gaze, eyebrows raised fearing rebuke or dislike, quick changing features	Firm contact but not constant, always direct when conveying a difficult or true message

(Continued)

93

Assertiveness

	Aggressive	Non-assertive	Assertive
Gestures	Head in the air, speaking to the hand, single and double fingers pointed up, "the pointed gun," arm thrusts, chin tilts, fist thumping, waving hands, the beating baton, shaking fists, leg-swinging, striding around impatiently, arms crossed, unapproachable	Hand wringing, hunched shoulders, covering the mouth with the hand, tapping of fingers, self-caressing	Hand movements are measured, firm, open and encouraging for others to become involved
Proximity	Entering others' space freely and frequently, no respect for personal space, prodding the person, leaning excessively forward	Conceding too much space with others', retreating, being sideways on, using physical barriers for protection	Respecting personal space, (dependent on situational factors – roughly arm's length)

Interpreting the non-verbal signals

It's easy to play amateur psychologist once you know a little about non-verbal behaviour; but here we'd like to lay down a few words of caution.

Back in the 1980s, we both went on a sales course that "taught" the participants how to correctly interpret body language, such as:

- If someone was listening to you with folded arms they were being defensive or resistant.
- If someone refused to give you eye contact they were being devious or shifty.
- A couple of nervous coughs before someone spoke or during the conversation was an indication they were likely to lie.
- The limp wrist, wet fish handshake was a sure sign of weakness or non-assertion; the anvil like grip a sign of strength and dominance.

Many people naturally sit with their arms folded – in some instances, this could be interpreted as closed behaviour, but they may in fact be fully attentive and responsive. It is their most relaxed and, in some cases, their most receptive and comfortable way to listen.

To take another example, some people genuinely find it very difficult to give you eye contact but this does not necessarily mean that you should not be able to trust their words.

Imagine you have shaken the hand of someone with a vice-like grip. You may assume them to be as equally strong when it comes to standing up for their views, but you could find instead that they are weak. Equally, you may have shaken hands with someone who has the grip of a wet fish, yet then found the person to be incredibly strong minded and courageous.

Clearly, body language affects us enormously and a single element of body language is not a predictive indicator of how someone else is thinking or feeling.

You can, however, form a rough opinion of their emotions and intentions if you observe a number of elements of body language that seem to suggest how people are feeling – providing you are also clear what is normal for that person.

1. Look for clusters of non-verbal behaviours

If you were speaking with someone and they begin to fold their arms, their face and jaw tightens up, and their posture becomes more rigid, something is changing and this *may be* an indication of resistance.

Body language comes in clusters of signals and postures, depending on the internal emotions and mental states. Recognizing a whole cluster is thus far more reliable than trying to interpret individual elements.

However, in the example above, it's still not possible to be sure whether these are signs of defensiveness because you don't know "what is normal" for this individual.

2. Calibrate what is normal

You need to calibrate these non-verbal behaviours with other non-verbal behaviours you have observed when you know the person had previously been defensive. Folded arms, stiffening of posture etc. may be representative of defensiveness for some, but maybe not for this particular individual.

Remember that body language varies greatly with people and, especially, between cultures – so be careful when applying local interpretations of body language to other cultures.

For instance, we were based in Fiji for a number of years and "taught" management skills to ethnic Fijians, Indians, Chinese and other South Pacific nationals. All hierarchical types of culture.

We soon learnt that lack of eye contact was not a sign of disrespect or disinterest but a deeply felt way of showing respect to seniority or status.

We found that in the Fijian culture it was disrespectful to talk to someone who was your senior in an authoritative tone when directing them or, even worse, disciplining them.

This proved an enormous challenge to younger, more educated Fijian managers trained in western management techniques, who were being asked to manage industrial and commercial businesses in a way contrary to their cultural norms. It was difficult for the young Fijians to give an instruction to a member of their village who was an elder or senior to them in the village pecking order, but not senior to them in their commercial hierarchy. The way they managed the conflict was to give instructions with their eyes averted and in soft apologetic tones – not the assertive way they had been taught!

Non face-to-face communication

We have talked a lot about face-to-face communication and that meaning sometimes has nothing to do with the actual words you are using.

How then can you get your message across clearly, if you can't use body language?

Both with written communication and on the telephone you are denied, to varying degrees, a number of non-verbal elements that aid effective communication. This has implications for building relationships, clarity and understanding.

But the good news is that you still have your voice.

As you will see there are a number of ways to militate against this by using our voice on the telephone and by using a communication tool we'll introduce shortly called "testing understanding." We have to accept that we are at a disadvantage.

On the telephone
When you are on the telephone or your mobile, you cannot see the other person (unless you use face recognition technology), but you

can experience them through the non-verbal behaviours associated with voice, tone, volume, speed and so on.

As much as possible, plan what you are going to say so that you can put more of your focus into listening and the way you use your voice. Too often on the phone your mind is so busy working out what to say next that you are not really paying attention to your tone.

Aspects of our body language, which you would normally show visually, such as attentiveness, humour and warmth now need to be communicated by voice tone, pace and volume, speed and emphasis.

Avoid speaking in a monotone unless you wish to match the other person's tone in order to build initial rapport. Vary the tone of your voice, up and down and emphasize words that you believe are important to making your point and which are of interest to the listener.

Should you wish to build rapport over the telephone you will be interested in three little words, *match*, *pace* and *lead* which, from our experience, works very well in building rapport.

- *Match* = matching tone, volume, emphasis, speed which allows you in some way to "sound" like them.
- *Pace* = matching the mood and emotion. This tells the other person you are working at their emotional level.
- *Lead* = once you sense you are in rapport, you can vary your speed, volume as to how you want to speak. For instance, you might slow down when explaining anything detailed, or speed up to show your excitement or enthusiasm. If you have matched enough the other person would normally take up your lead and match your tone, speed and so on. If this doesn't happen, you will need to match and pace a little longer as you have not established rapport solidly enough yet.

Some examples of the match–pace–lead process

- If the other person speaks slowly and deliberately, so do you.
- If they speak in short sentences – so do you.
- If they speak quietly and softly and with little emphasis – so do you.
- If they sound chirpy and enthusiastic – so do you, and so on.

Customer service representatives and sales people are encouraged to smile when they talk on the phone – the smile comes over in the warmth and the texture of the voice.

Try it the next time you are on the phone and see what a difference it makes. Imagine the person is in front of you and you want them to understand fully what you are saying.

When you make that next difficult telephone call, set yourself in the assertive position, and feel the confidence it gives you to communicate in a firm, fair and open way.

Testing (*YOUR*) understanding

Unless you have face recognition you cannot see if what you are saying is understood by the other party, or the effect it has on them. As we have discussed, you can get some inkling by tuning in to the other person's voice, tone and so on. Some people, however, give very little reaction over the phone, so even then it can be difficult to work out whether you and they have understanding or agreement.

Testing your understanding is a potent verbal tool in most circumstances, and using it over the phone maximizes clarity and understanding and also builds rapport.

One of the ways to be clear throughout a phone conversation is to periodically check your understanding that you have correctly interpreted what the other party has said.

Using testing understanding builds:

- *rapport* – it demonstrates that you have listened;
- *confidence* – you are on the same wavelength;
- *agreement* – if you have misheard, or misinterpreted, now is your chance to get it right. And much better to do it sooner rather than try to build agreement on shifting sand.

An example of a testing understanding question would be during a conversation with Michelle where a number of options have been discussed. You could clarify exactly what has been agreed by testing your understanding: "Michelle, are you saying you are now fine with the arrangements for tomorrow night and we'll meet at the cinema entrance?"

Written communication

Vocal tone is hard to distinguish in written materials compared to talking face-to-face. You have to be much more careful with the choice of words and phrasing. You may have written something seemingly innocuous only to find out that it has been taken entirely the wrong way. "I want you to be careful in this instance" may have been a statement of your concern and care. It may have been a thoroughly good piece of advice, but is taken by the receiver as an admonition and a suspicion that you think the person has not been careful in the past – a suggestion to pull their socks up!

With any written communication it's important to remember that information needs to be presented clearly and concisely. In order to avoid confusion and misunderstanding about your emotions, you must be careful what you write and how you write it.

Body language, tone of voice and other factors completely change the meaning of a few words, and they don't translate to email, texts, letters or reports.

Body language is not a factor in written communication, so your intentions may be ambiguous if you are not clear. You may use "smileys" and "emoticons" but they may not appropriately represent your emotions or, by using them, you may be seen as someone who is not professional or doesn't want to be taken seriously.

In addition, the way you use punctuation, spaces, underlining and emphasis – as well as the use of bold and italics – will affect the reader's perception, and not necessarily in the way you had hoped.

Ever had an email from someone who believes CAPITALS ARE THE WAY TO GET EVERYONE'S ATTENTION – liberally sprinkled, of course, with a number of exclamation marks?!?!

SURELY YOU HAVE COME ACROSS THIS *MANY TIMES* IN YOUR LIFE BEFORE!!!

The result is that you tend to feel shouted at.

Ever read a report that is like a concrete block of writing? Long-winded sentences with few full stops, thousands of commas, no paragraphs or indentations, nothing to break up the intensity of what has been written whilst it relates one idea to another – or not in some cases – because, by the time you get to the end of the sentence, it is very hard, or at least sometimes it seems too hard to remember the beginning of the sentence, or some of the important messages in the middle, before you can piece together the meaning at the end.

Imagine page after page like this – would you look forward to reading it with wild, exuberant desire, or with dread?

Even in the world of *words* non-verbal behaviour has implications for understanding impact and influence.

Earlier, when discussing how to build trust and confidence on the phone, we mentioned rapport, the desire to stand in another's shoes so you can build communication bridges. We tend to gravitate towards those who are like us. Let us now look at the benefits of rapport in a number of situations one of which would be, as we have seen, over the phone.

Trust and rapport

Most people work best with people they know and trust. If you trust someone, they know you have their interests at heart, and that you will consider their needs, opinions and ideas. This does not mean necessarily you will agree with them, but they feel confident that they will be heard, and their needs acknowledged.

Think of those people who are most dear to you, or you really like to hang out with or you find it easy to communicate with. Do you have things in common with them or are they completely different to you?

Contrast with people you don't get on with, or you wouldn't want to hang out with or with whom you find it difficult to talk. Are they similar to you, or different?

We tend to hang out with people with whom we have things in common and we look for common interests and experiences when forming relationships.

Where we share something in common we feel a mutual bond. When we first meet people we will often search for those commonalities by asking questions, "where do you live . . . what do you do?" and, when we find something similar, we feel more secure and confident talking to them and with them.

People like people who are similar to themselves, or who they aspire to become. Have you ever met a perfect stranger and yet felt instantly comfortable with them? As if you've known them for ages. You've found rapport!

On the other hand, have you ever met someone for the first time and instantly disliked them or felt uncomfortable with them for no apparent reason? You probably have little in common and have to work hard at the relationship and at the communication process.

What is rapport?

Rapport is based on the idea that people who are similar to one another will like each other. This can be defined in a number of ways:

* A state between two or more people that precedes influence.
* Sharing a personal chemistry with one or more people.
* A co-operative relationship.
* Being on the same wavelength as someone else.
* Being in tune with each other.
* Seeing things the same way.
* A like-mindedness.

Creating rapport is not the outcome of our communication, but a process rather than a state.

Have you ever been at a dinner party where you have turned to the person next to you and found that, for a while, you have a wonderful, easy conversation? Then, gradually, conversation dries up and you turn to the person on the other side of you and start all over again, sometimes successfully and sometimes not.

Benefits of rapport

The following list is by no means exhaustive, but illustrates some of the practical and communication reasons why building rapport is so useful.

- You never get a second chance to make a first impression so you want to create the impact you want.
- You want what you say to be memorable, and influence the other party.
- You want to leave people with the sense that being with you has been a pleasurable, positive and helpful experience.
- You want people to see you again, and to remember you as someone who listens, understands and shows respect.
- If people have had positive experiences from being with you they are more likely to do a favour when needed and give you the benefit of the doubt if misunderstandings occur.
- As well as understanding others you want others to understand you and to buy in to your ideas, opinions and needs.
- Building rapport builds trust, and with trust anything is possible.
- Once you have established rapport, he or she is more likely to be open with you, share information and support your ideas.

How do I know I have rapport?

One visible sign of being in rapport is the extent to which each person is mirroring or reflecting aspects of the other person's behaviour. When people are in rapport they mirror each other's movements, reflecting verbal and non-verbal behaviours (discussed previously) such as similar posture, ways of talking, tone of voice, and the mood that exists between them. One "golden test" you could look out for is when silence feels comfortable; nothing is being said but there is no awkwardness.

Rapport between two people can be likened to a dance: one person follows the other in a rhythmic embrace. When you have rapport, both parties follow each other's cues, and it does not seem to matter who is leading and who is following. As one person changes, so does the other.

As we have said, it's easy to have rapport with people who we like and respect, and with whom we share the same values, interests, beliefs and experiences. It is, on the face of it, easier to listen in these situations, although unless we decide to listen we may fall into the poor listening habits we discussed before. What about other situations when we don't admire, like and respect the other person?

Establishing rapport where there seems to be little or nothing in common

At work, normally, we don't choose our colleagues, peers and so on, yet we have to work with them constructively on a daily basis. They are instrumental in helping us achieve our goals and vice versa. There are many social contexts where we need to work with people with whom we don't necessarily get on.

There are times when we may have much in common with other people, but still we don't get on with them. We may have similar ideas, beliefs and experiences, but it is neither compulsory nor a done deal that we will get on with them.

Whether you like someone or not you can still respect them. This does not mean kowtowing to them or having to agree with what they say or do.

Whether you like them or not you can still have rapport with them.

It is fallacious to think that other people experience the world as you do. There is no right view; rapport is about having a common view not a right one.

You can build rapport with people at many levels.

You can build rapport at a non-verbal level by being in sync with others' non-verbal behaviours, for example by using the communication process discussed earlier: match, pace, lead.

Showing respect through assertive listening is a lower risk strategy than matching. Matching, if not done with the right attention, elegance and subtlety, can be construed as mimicking.

Assertive listening allows you to reap the rewards of rapport building by demonstrating that even though you may have different beliefs, experiences and ways of looking at life, the other person's views, however different, are nonetheless valid and valued.

With assertive listening, you can celebrate the difference whilst adding to your knowledge, experience, tolerance, understanding and value of human kind.

As one of Suzanne's old bosses said to me, "If you and I are always in agreement and see things in similar fashion, one of us is redundant!" Viva la Difference!

No interaction with another individual is neutral – it's either for *better* or *worse*. You choose!

You may not always want to be in rapport with someone, you may want to break rapport to establish certain positions or views – as in the following example – but you never want to suspend the process of active listening.

Jo – master of rapport

Jo's life in selling was a mixed blessing. No one was faster at establishing rapport with the clients. Clients loved working with Jo and, as it happened, seemed to get better deals from Jo than from the other sales people.

And Jo loved to spend time with customers, feeling easy and comfortable in their presence, until it came to closing the deal and talking about price.

The customers would then pull on Jo's heart strings and, being so in tune with the client, Jo didn't want to upset the apple cart, stand up for the company or achieve a win-win for everyone.

What Jo needed to do (and eventually managed to do) was to break rapport with the customer when price was being discussed. Jo could then have an independent state of mind that would allow a negotiation for the best deal for everyone.

To be successful at building rapport requires you to develop a curiosity and genuine interest in other people's views, opinions and needs. Once rapport is established, it creates an atmosphere of trust. Rapport facilitates a greater openness to exploring areas of mutuality when *prima facie* individual needs suggest they are in conflict. You have already sown the seeds of cooperation and can build on this mood music to negotiate win-win.

You may not feel skilled enough or feel authentic enough when you modify your non-verbal behaviours as in match, pace, lead; or accommodate interest or values different to your own; or have common experiences – but there are always reasons a plenty to really listen to someone else.

The most practical way we show that others are valued is by actively and assertively listening to them. Assertive listening allows you to show, despite the other differences, that the other person is valued in the deepest possible way – a pre-requisite for establishing rapport with anyone.

Assertive listening

There are none so blind as those that cannot see, and none so deaf as those that cannot hear.

Assertive listening demonstrates the desire to value and understand others' needs and opinions and shows respect. It is a major gateway to creating rapport.

Think back to a time when you first became interested in someone else. For instance, perhaps it was the first time you were going out with your spouse or partner or someone who has since become a very valued friend. No doubt you will recall you were very interested in them and wanted to let them know that's how you felt and how important they were to you.

In some cases you'd hang on their every word and, when it was reciprocated, you felt you were valued and your ideas and opinions were listened to. It became easy to be in that person's company and speak to them. Gradually you were able to discuss your more intimate thoughts and ideas. Strong bonds between the two of you began to be established and cemented. Everybody else can see you are getting along witnessed by the way your behaviour mirrors or matches each other. Both parties are engaged in an empathetic dance.

Contrast that with the ending of the relationship, when the fire and the magic has gone, when the caring, loving and interest has waned and absent. You will notice the first thing to disappear from the relationship is the ability to listen to each other. Indeed, it may be one of the barbs that are tossed out like hand grenades between you: "you no longer listen," followed by . . . "that's because you don't care anymore."

And the dance that was so fluid has turned into a battle, with neither party even able to look into each other's faces or make eye contact and, where before there was symmetry, there is now difference and absence.

Assertive listening is central to relationships and one of the core ways to demonstrate to others they are valued and respected. It is key to building trust.

Win-win involves an exploration of the needs of both parties. This will involve probing skills and the ability to listen assertively – not only to the factual content but also to the emotional needs expressed.

If you are too busy with your own thoughts and needs you completely miss the cues and markers that can lead to a win-win solution.

There are those that hear.

There are those that wait to talk.

There are those that listen.

Which one are you?

You have to *decide* to listen or, too quickly, you enter a Walter Mitty world where, whilst someone is talking to you, you indulge in fantastic daydreams of your own, fantasizing about yourself, and what you'd say or do.

You do not exist in a vacuum and, when you are involved in any negotiation, you can't help but give out all sorts of clues and markers about how you feel, what you want and where the ground is fertile for win-win opportunities.

The goals of assertive listening are:

1. To let others know that you want to understand their point of view.
2. To understand accurately what someone else is saying.
3. To let others know that they have been understood.

The low reactor boss
Ben, a production manager, invited me to observe a typical meeting with one of his staff, Sally.

Both had been finding it increasingly difficult to get on and communication between them was particularly sticky.

Working with both it soon became apparent that Ben's listening skills were a major obstacle to creating a good working relationship.

During a conversation with Sally, Ben's face was deadpan and expressionless. It didn't take long before Ben's eyes seemed to glaze over as he stared into the distance and out through the windows of his office.

As a consequence, the conversation between Ben and Sally was stilted. Sally had hoped for a lively debate on the pros and cons of her suggestion but, instead, had received little or no reaction. Consequently, she had tried different ways to make the same point, in the hope she would elicit a reaction. What seemed to incense Sally most was how quickly Ben lost interest and gazed out of the window.

So, by the end of a conversation, Sally walked out bemused and annoyed at the lack of interaction. Sally thought Ben rude, bordering on the arrogant, with little time and interest for her and her ideas.

After a conversation with Ben, I asked him what he thought of the conversation. Remarkably, Ben was able to repeat verbatim everything Sally had said. Apparently his looking out of the window was misinterpreted as lack of interest whereas that was Ben's way of concentrating on Sally's ideas.

So, clearly, although Ben may have been taking it all in, he was not *demonstrating* he was listening – he had become in communication terms a "low reactor."

Until he changed and became more active in his listening, Sally's perception of him as being rude, arrogant and disinterested would be reconfirmed each time they met.

As this true story demonstrates, it is not enough just to listen – you have to *demonstrate* you are listening. Or you invite stumbling, repetition, stuttering from the speaker, going around whilst creating a perception in others that you are arrogant, rude, uncaring and self-absorbed.

This kind of conversation is not only confined to the business world, it is equally familiar in social and family situations where one party is intent on explaining something whilst the other is preoccupied with themselves. Maybe they emit the odd grunt or lightning quick glance, while the other person goes on and on relentlessly. The party not listened to then realizes that talking is an unrewarding activity and limits their level of response to as few words as possible.

So the important thing is to make our listening assertive by:

- demonstrating that we are actively listening through our verbal and non-verbal responses, and
- showing that we understand what's being said to us by summarizing or testing our understanding, for example: "that must have come as quite a surprise and I can see that it would cause you embarrassment."

Ways of showing you are listening

It is not enough just to listen: you need to show that you are giving the other person your attention. There are a number of ways you can do it – we'll look at both some non-verbal and verbal ways.

First, though, there are a number of general points worth noting about assertive listening:

- Assertive listening on your part encourages others to listen to you. The law of reciprocity works: if you are interested in me, I'll be interested in you and, of course, it works the other way as well.

- The display of listening needs to be active not passive: it is the *enabling* role, and the more genuinely active you are in listening the better. Seeing your reaction is a way that other people can measure that you *are* listening. Until we refine the art of telepathy that is all you and I have.
- If you feel you are being listened to, you feel relaxed and more open. If you are tense, you allow your thoughts to race around and it is hard to give attention to the other person.

  If you find yourself doing so, take a few deep breaths, relax and clear your mind.
- Allow people to complete what they are saying rather than interrupting and finishing off their sentences, jumping the gun or assuming you know what they are going to say. Very often, the real part of the message will come at the end.
- Ask questions as they come up. Especially if the answers are important to understanding the other person's position.

Assertive listening through our body language

You cannot *not* communicate. Even when you do not *say anything*, you are still communicating. So communicate positively through your body language. Ways of doing this include the following:

- **Posture.** The best posture to have in a situation like this is a relaxed one, generally upright or moving towards the person you are listening to.
- **Gestures.** These are open and generally low, at waist height.
- **Facial expression.** This will be open, enquiring and generally mirroring the other person's expression when appropriate. Nod your head by all means, but avoid the nodding dog syndrome at all costs.
- **Eye contact.** When you talk to people, look at them directly. When you do this, you show them that you're giving them your undivided attention. However, constant eye contact may sometimes be interpreted as aggression. You can then look

away just for a moment to indicate that you are thinking about what they've said before you look at them to respond.

- **Space and proximity.** We generally feel comfortable when we have about twenty three inches of personal space around us – like a magic force field – and feel threatened when this space is closed down. Allow people their personal space.
- **Use of silence and pausing.** Allow people to finish off their own sentences and don't jump in – pausing and silence will encourage people to talk more easily.
- **Use of emphatics.** These are the grunting sounds – the "um" and "er" type noises that are so encouraging and help to maintain the flow of the conversation.

Assertive listening by summarizing

You can give people immediate evidence that you've heard them by summarizing what you believe has been said or agreed.

"So you believe that I'm not paying you and the kids enough attention because, if I was, I'd be home from work earlier?"

"So, just to conclude, we have all put our ideas forward for increasing our charity giving."

"Nial, you're going way to explore government funding whilst Jamal and Bella are going to concentrate on beefing up our lottery bid; the rest of us are responsible for contacting those charities who expressed an interest in us last year."

Assertive listening by testing understanding

You can let others know you are interested in understanding their points of view in by using such phrases as:

"I'm interested to find out your views on . . ."

"I'd like to understand what you think about . . ."

"Could you tell me how you feel about this . . .?"

"What does the problem or issue look like from your point of view?"

"I'm curious to know more about your opinion on . . ."

When you use these phrases it is important to demonstrate with your body language that you are generally interested and want to understand the other person's point of view. You can do this by using good eye contact, leaning slightly forward to express interest, keeping a relaxed open posture and indicating with your gestures that you would like to hear more.

Behaviour is catching

The sense that assertiveness is about influence and persuasion is palpably true. Assertiveness is not about force but about personal strength and flexibility.

Behaviour is catching.

When someone is nasty or uncooperative towards you, the tendency is to be nasty or uncooperative back. When someone is kind and respectful towards you the tendency is to reciprocate.

If someone is aggressive towards you, the knee jerk reaction is to be aggressive in return. However, if you respond in an assertive way it is unlikely that you will be met with assertion immediately. The aggression may even intensify as the person concerned is not getting the reaction they are used to. However, if you maintain your assertion, the person being aggressive has to move towards being assertive in order to maintain the conversation.

Whoever maintains their state of mind and behaviour the longest will win out.

When someone is behaving aggressively or non-assertively towards you, know that maintaining an assertive stance will bring about the best result. In these situations, you need to hold on to your assertive behaviour especially under persistent pressure.

If you want things to come out the way you think they should, *you* are probably the best person to improve the chances that they will. By taking responsibility you gain the *right* to influence the outcome. You also need some tools to help you do so; that way you can keep calm, maintain your psychological state, and encourage the other person to catch your assertive behaviour.

Levels of assertive options

We face a variety of situations involving quite different people and, if we are to be effective, we need a wide range of assertive options. The aim of assertive communication is to get your point across clearly, without confusion or misunderstanding, and so you need to communicate in a way that is congruent.

When you add the variations possible with non-verbal behaviour you have an infinite number of ways to respond.

The figure on the following page is a pyramid of seven assertive options.

The bottom three are day-to-day behaviours. The top four options are to be used as the situation you are dealing with becomes more difficult and extreme. You might decide to work your way slowly up the pyramid until you have a satisfactory resolution. When using assertive techniques it is worth planning them and anticipating other people's behaviour and preparing your possible responses.

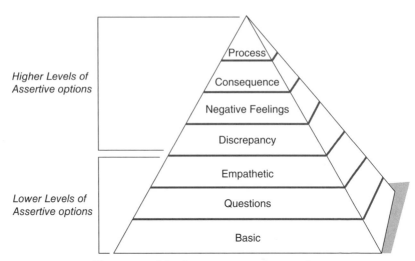

The pyramid of seven assertive options

The three *Lower Levels of Assertive options* cover the majority of day-to-day situations we encounter. You can use them in various combinations where you need to express your own needs and want to ensure others' needs and feelings are considered.

If you have used the lower levels to no effect then use *Higher Levels of Assertion*. This will give you further flexibility whilst still respecting the other person's position. You will also show, by doing this, your determination to resolve the issue.

We suggest you keep the levels as low as possible and certainly start with the lower levels or you will be perceived as "going to war" over every little thing.

In addition, if you start at the higher levels of assertion and you are not successful you have used up your options if you wish to escalate further.

Lower levels of assertion

1. Basic assertion

A straightforward statement about your opinions, feelings or needs. Make sure you have the facts and information you need to hand. At this level, it is preferable to express yourself in "I" language form, using "we" when that is appropriate.

For example:

"I believe this to be the case . . ."
"As I see the situation . . ."
"In my view . . ."
"I suggest that we go for . . ."
"I see it differently . . ."
"I'd prefer to do this"
"I'd rather not do that . . ."
"We all need to consider our options."

2. Questions assertion

Asking questions to try to understand another person's perspective and situation.

For example:

"What would you prefer to do?"
"How do you see it?"
"What ideas do you have?"
"What makes you say that?"
"I would like your ideas on this?"
"How would we get round this?"
"What difficulties does this create?"
"Are you saying that?"

3. Empathy assertion

Combining a show of understanding with a statement of your needs or opinion.

Avoid *but* or *however* when making an empathy statement.

The use of these conjunctions is seen to be disingenuous, for example, "I don't want to pick holes in what you said *but* I think you are wrong." What most of us will hear is, "but I think you're wrong" and dismiss the rest.

The words *but* or *however*, normally discount the empathetic statement that has gone before, and people dismiss the empathic intent. As a dear friend once told us, "It's what goes after the *but* that folks really mean, the bit before is just bull!"

"And" is an adding word which you can substitute for *but* and restore the impact of showing empathy.

Another way to do this is to remove the *but* completely and uncouple the empathy statement from the rest, allowing a gap or a pause between the show of empathy and what you still need, as in the first example below.

For example:

> "Sarah, I appreciate you need to leave early this evening. I still need your help to finish these figures by the end of today."
> PAUSE/GAP
> "I do think the job you are doing is very difficult. I still need to spend more time understanding their situation."
> "I know you are anxious to transfer to another department as soon as you can. I still need you to give 100% + to the Vodax Account."

"Yes, that customer sounded very rude. They still need our help to deliver the best service we can."

Exercise – Experimenting with the lower levels of assertion

Experiment with the lower levels of assertion to achieve various outcomes.

Practise out loud the examples below.

1. Basic Assertion

1. "I feel very strongly or passionately about."
2. "I feel committed to that."
3. "I have no preference one way or the other."
4. "I don't agree or want to do that."
5. "I strongly disagree or definitely don't want to do that."

How accurately are you expressing the strength of what you think, want, feel?

2. Questions Assertion

Try out some questions, particularly ones you find more difficult to ask. For example:

- "Exactly when will it be ready?"
- "Are you sure it's the real problem?"
- "Can you really guarantee that it will be ready on Monday?"

Do you really want to know the answer? How much are you finding out where others really stand?

(*Continued*)

119

3. Empathy Assertion

Try out some empathy. For example:

* "I can see you're unhappy with the present arrangement. I still need your support whilst we search for another solution."

Is your empathy genuinely received?

Higher levels of assertion

When people consistently and persistently seem to ignore our needs and opinions, we need to stand up for our needs in a firmer way whilst still respecting the rights of the other person.

4. Discrepancy Assertion

A statement which points out the difference between what was previously agreed and what is actually happening, or about to happen, and expresses what you want to happen.

"John, as I remember, we agreed that you would loan me one of your staff to help meet these deadlines.

"Now you're saying you haven't got anyone available.

"I want to stick to our original agreement."

5. Negative Feelings Assertion

A statement drawing attention to the undesirable effect someone else's behaviour is having on you. Be careful not to blame them for your feelings! Use "I" not "You."

A useful structure to guide your negative feeling assertion is:

* "*When you . . .*" (describe their behaviour)
* "*The effects are . . .*" (how their behaviour affects you/others)
* "*I feel . . .*" (how you feel about this)
* "*I'd like . . .*" (what you want them to do differently)

It's important to "own" your feelings (e.g. "*I feel angry*") as opposed to blaming others for the way you feel ("*you made me feel . . .*")

"Brian, at the end of team meetings, you invariably want to have the last word and go over ground we have already covered and agreed. I am becoming more and more frustrated when you do this as it means we spend extra time revisiting what we have already agreed. I need you to make your point at the appropriate time in future."

Or

"When you make decisions on my behalf I feel slightly undermined. I'd rather feel confident you trusted me in future . . ."

6. Sanctions Assertion

Informing the other person of the consequences for them if they don't change their behaviour. Make sure you give them an opportunity to then change their behaviour.

The "sanction" needs to be:

* one that you have the right to carry out;
* are prepared to carry it out; and
* within your own circle of influence and discretion.

"Susan, if you don't supply us with the information we need to do our jobs, I will have to tell the board that we cannot meet their deadline.

"I'd rather not have to do that.

"So let's now reach agreement on this."

7. Process Assertion

There may be exceptional times when none of the assertive options above seem to work. The other person remains, angry, obdurate, unwilling and there is an element of *déjà vu* the next time you meet and discuss the same or another issue.

Normally something else is "going on," which often has nothing to do with the current conversation; it may not even directly be related to you.

(Continued)

121

There is a *hidden agenda* at play and until you challenge and explore what it is, it remains a silent obstacle.

> "Nigel, it's not like you to be negative and angry over the slightest error and then totally ignore what we have to say. I am curious to know what's really going on for you at the moment?
>
> "Can we talk about that and then return to the issue?"

You return home from work and, almost before you've closed the door, you find that your partner seems to want to get into a serious argument over what seems trivial. You are a bit stunned and taken aback at the outburst from nowhere.

> "Mal, I know we are arguing about me giving you short notice about going out tonight, but I sense there is something else on your mind, maybe about something I've said or done recently. If there is, can we talk about it?"

Exercise: Higher levels of assertion

Write down some examples of your own and practise saying them out loud.

Discrepancy Assertion

_____

_____

Negative Feelings Assertion

_____

_____

Process Assertion

_____

_____

Exercise: To establish what your current assertive communication style is like

We are going to do an exercise in your imagination:

1. Write down as many words as you can to complete the phrase:

"When I am being assertive I am . . ."

(answers might be: confident, relaxed, authoritative, in control, etc.)

2. Think of a time from your past when you were like this.

Think about what you wanted and what you achieved.

3. In your mind's eye go back to that situation and see yourself there *now* and write down the answers to the following questions.
   - What words or phrases are you using?
   - How are you feeling?
   - How are you using your voice?
   - What is the volume like?
   - What is your tone of voice like?
   - How fast or slow are you speaking?
   - What words or phrases are you putting emphasis on?
   - How are you using silence and pausing?
   - How are you standing or sitting and your general movement?
   - What gestures are you using and how are you using your hands?
   - How open and relaxed is your face and facial expression?
   - How constant or fleeting is your eye contact?
   - How is your assertive communication influencing the other person(s)?
   - What is the other person's reaction and how are you managing that reaction?

(Continued)

If you do this exercise and get a representation of your assertive non-verbal communication you will have a very useful template of "how you are" when you are assertive.

Every time you reproduce this template, you increase the chances that you'll achieve a similar result in other situations you face in life.

Summary

The measure of how effective you are in your communication rests largely with you. You measure the effectiveness of your communication by the response you get. If you are not getting the response you want you need to change the way you are communicating. If you always do what you've always done you'll always get what you always got. Flexibility is the key.

You are responsible. This can only be good news because we can't really be responsible for other people's behaviour – so we may as well concentrate on our own. You don't have to ask anyone for permission to do something else. Do it – be alive to the reaction and feedback and celebrate or adjust accordingly.

PART TWO

Welcome to Part Two of this book, which illustrates how you can make use of all the assertive tools and techniques discussed so far in this book.

Assertiveness is beneficial in all the roles we play in our life – as a parent, partner, friend, colleague, manager.

We have deliberately chosen social and work-related situations that prove challenging to most people where you can see how assertive behaviour can make you more effective and confident and, ultimately, have a more fulfilling life.

You will get most from this section if you apply your own tricky situations and relationships to the scenarios illustrated. Below is a list of the various features used throughout. These will provide you with the key elements to pay attention to in order to become more assertive. There are also exercises to complete at the end of each chapter, to help you to become more assertive in an increasing number of situations in your life.

A real-life story

Each chapter starts with a true-life story of an event that participants on our courses have related to us. There's likely to be a familiar ring to the tale because you've experienced something similar.

Wake-up call

The events described in the real-life story don't just happen out of the blue. There is a build-up until the alarm bells ring and indicate that something has to change in your life. At this point, you'll be given some of the clues that suggest you've arrived at this "wake-up" stage.

Standing in the other person's/people's shoes . . . what are they thinking?

At this point, you'll be asked to consider: what's the pay-off for others to continue their behaviour? And, as a consequence, what could they be saying to themselves? When you understand someone else's position and what drives their behaviour you have more information on which to base your actions. It also helps you build rapport with them because you can demonstrate greater understanding.

Taking things on when they're small

We have an increased chance of handling problems successfully when they're small, as opposed to allowing them to grow much bigger and then requiring a super human effort to resolve them. This is where you'll be asked to face up to reality and be honest with yourself about what's been going on for you.

Options

You'll be prompted to ask yourself what would be an assertive mindset for you to move forward with. You can choose realistic and pro-active conversations to take place inside your head. Most importantly you can think about win-win outcomes.

You can also choose to adopt more balanced assertive beliefs about your skills and abilities and you'll be encouraged to review what others are capable of too.

The options will also remind you that you can allow yourself permission to tackle a particular situation assertively, by asserting your rights.

Actions

Here we'll describe the specific behaviours for you to adopt, and present the assertive language for you to use with others, in order to bring about the changes you desire.

Time to choose

Finally, there will be an exercise where you can relate a situation of your own to the one described. Think about your situation and write yourself an action plan based on the following questions:

- What specifically are you going to do?
- When will you start it?
- What might be potential barriers to stop you doing it?
- What aspects of this book can help you most in overcoming potential barriers?
- Whose help do you need to support you?
- How will you reward yourself?

Now begin!

No matter how much theory you learn, no matter how well you plan, you will discover your true potential and enhance your assertive skills when you integrate these concepts and techniques into your daily life. Build on what you've learnt and complete the exercises at the end of each chapter to lay the foundations for your assertive future.

> *Whatever you can do, or dream you can do, begin it.*
> *Boldness has genius, power and magic in it.*
> *So begin it now.*
>
> William Hutchinson Murray

5
Getting the Respect You Deserve at Work

Saying "no," handling put-downs and being taken seriously

A real-life story

A client, Bill, has been using your services for four months now as part of a six-month trial period. Signing this contract with such a high profile account was a real coup for your boss and could produce significant revenue for your company.

However, each month, Bill exceeds the hours he's being billed for and you know everyone's afraid to say "no" when he requests further changes.

You've just handled a difficult telephone call with Bill when Jane, your boss' PA, says rather irritatingly "the trouble with you is you're just far too nice, you should let them know who's boss."

Your team is asked to come up with ideas for working more efficiently with Bill because the workload is increasing and fast becoming unmanageable for everyone. You have made a couple of suggestions, such as increasing the headcount on a temporary basis and targeting high value accounts. These suggestions have just been ignored by other members of the team.

You're about to leave the office for an offsite lunch meeting with Bill when Max, a member of your staff, who has a habit of putting people down and being sarcastic says, "off on a jolly are you?"

 # Wake-up call

Is this happening more and more frequently?

- The atmosphere in the office becomes stressful when a new client is taken on.
- Everyone's afraid to say "no" to extra requests.
- The office banter has more of an edge.
- You're becoming more reluctant to speak up and offer any ideas.

- Rarely are your ideas taken seriously.
- The same individual puts people down.
- There's growing resentment towards management.

Standing in the other person's shoes

What might Bill be saying to himself?

- "They clearly think these extras are in the contract."
- "They must be short of clients. I wonder how much more I can get out of them?"
- "A nice guy but he's a bit soft and a real push over."

What might other team members being saying to themselves?

- "Always being conciliatory does none of us any favours."
- "He needs to stand up for himself and the company's interests more."
- "Why doesn't he present his views with more enthusiasm and commitment?"
- "If he doesn't believe in his ideas why should we?"
- "I wish he would say more clearly exactly what he wants to happen."

Taking things on when they're small

What in the past have you allowed to happen? Does any of this sound familiar?

- Your first response always seems to be "yes."
- You need to be seen as helpful and want all your relationships to be friendly all of the time.
- The knots in your stomach seem to grow each time you face possible conflict.

- You've found it easier to give in than stick up for yourself.
- You just accept things rather than challenge or ask questions.
- You've just backed down when you feel your ideas are under attack.
- You've been getting more anxious and upset about work.
- You've allowed your workload to increase.
- You feel increasingly isolated and want to avoid others.
- You're feeling increasingly bad about yourself.

 ## Options

What mindset would be helpful?

- "I can stop and think and give myself time before responding."
- "I can explain to the client that these extras are not part of the contract."
- "I can say that I'm happy to do them and that they will be billed accordingly."
- "I can tell my staff that I will support them if they say no."
- "I can ask for my manager's support."
- "I can work smarter not harder."
- "I can stand up for myself and explain why I believe my ideas are valid."
- "I can be brief, direct and to the point when I explain things."
- "I can find out what benefit Max is getting from these put-downs."

What permission do you need to give yourself to tackle these situations assertively?

- I have the right to represent the company fairly.
- I have the right to the resources, including time, to do the job properly.

- I have the right to have my views heard.
- I have the right to receive feedback on my ideas and learn how to improve them.
- I have the right not to be ridiculed, whether it be in public or not.

What win-win outcomes are possible?

- As a business if we make sufficient profit: the customer will get a good service.
- If I present well thought through ideas: others will be keen to pay attention to them.
- I'll spend time with Max to understand his concerns: he'll feel more valued at work.

 ## Actions

Saying no

It's difficult. You want to be known as someone who is helpful, who will go the extra mile and generally has a can-do attitude. You may think saying no is a career limiting opportunity.

You can, however, easily sabotage your career by saying yes all the time. Your credibility and reputation can be irreparably damaged if you end up failing to deliver something you've committed to do.

Prioritizing is the first step to working smarter and knowing which tasks make the priority list and which don't. A part of prioritizing is to decide when to say no to tasks that do not need your full attention right now.

Saying no can help manage expectations, your work load, improve your work performance, and your relationships.

- Say no in a concise and committed way – (see Saying No exercise in Chapter 2).

- Stand your ground. If people get the impression that they can talk you round you will encourage them to be extra persistent until you give in.
- Be aware of your body language when you are saying something serious. Avoid nervous smiles.
- When you say "no" avoid nodding and saying "ok."
- Concentrate on pausing after you have heard another's point of view – this will give you time to think. It will also show others you are considerate and thinking carefully what they've just said.
- Use assertive language and avoid words such as "maybe" and "perhaps."

Clarify your expectations

Problems often occur in relationships when people have different expectations of each other that are not clarified. In our scenario, let us look at how you would clarify these expectations by using a range of assertive options.

1. Basic assertion *A statement of where you stand, your needs and wants.* You decide to approach Bill to manage/clarify his expectations.	"Bill (client), I wanted to talk to you about these extras we've been asked to do above what we agreed in the contract. From now on they need to be paid for separately as they are not a part of the provisional six month agreement . . ."
2. Question assertion *Encouraging and inviting a response from others.* You ask a question to encourage Bill to respond. *Bill resists . . .*	". . . What's your view on that?" *"Well, you've allowed this to happen and thereby have sanctioned it."*

(Continued)

3. Empathy assertion *Conveys recognition that you understand how others feel.* You respond to this by emphasizing with Bill.	"Bill, I appreciate this is the way you see it. "Can you see that I want to do the best we can for you and that I need to focus on our contractual obligations first?"
Bill is still persisting . . .	*"Well if you want to do the best you can, just keep giving us what we ask for."*
4. Discrepancy assertion *You refer back to a previous discussion or an implicit agreement between you.*	"Bill, as I remember, you wanted to work in a spirit of collaboration i.e. give and take. We have already done a number of extras and it seems that it is my company that is doing all the giving and you all the taking. I'd like us to go back to the original intention. How about you?"
Bill persists further. . .	*"Look, we chose your organization because you seemed more flexible than your competitors."*
5. Negative assertion *Feelings are an important part of personal influence and can often be the key to show implications on you and how you feel about them.*	"Bill, help me out here. I am disappointed and bemused that we can't agree on something that is fair and equitable. What do we have to do to get agreement?"
Bill persists further . . .	*"We want a fair working relationship too, but you should have told me there was a problem earlier – you've allowed our expectations to grow."*

6. Sanction assertion

Demonstrates your commitment to a solution and what you are personally prepared to do to bring about a win-win negotiation.

"I accept that and I'm largely to blame for not doing so.

"Moving forward we need to find a solution we're both happy with so we can progress with the project. Unless we can agree that "extras" are to be charged for separately I can't sanction any further ones. I don't want that to happen so let's agree a way forward."

This conversation may be resolved here.

If Bill continues to resist a win-win you can go to the process level to resolve.

"I'm still not happy about this and I don't see why I should have to start paying for stuff you've previously included."

7. Process assertion

Taking the issue offline – like a timeout – so positions can soften, and clarify if there are any underlying issues that are getting in the way of a solution.

Your emotional sensors indicate that there may be other reasons why Bill is so obdurate.

"Bill, it's unlike you to dig your heals in. It sounds like someone's putting you under a lot of pressure? What's going on?"

Handling put-downs

Put-downs can come at you out of the blue and with no warning. Have you ever had a put-down which you haven't been able to answer there and then?

Seconds later the perfect answer comes to you, but the moment has gone and so has the person.

Put-downs give you that sinking feeling in the pit of your stomach and your stomach keeps count until it can take no more and you explode with aggression.

Put-downs are things people say to you when they are feeling bad about themselves and want you to feel bad about yourself = I'm NOT OK and neither are YOU!

Striking back with your own put-downs may feel good but is often a pre-cursor to spiralling retaliation. The person who has put you down knows they have got through because you react.

The purpose of handling put-downs is to *stop them* and do it in a way that *maintains your self-respect*.

Not reacting

One of the options is not to react (denying them the reaction they want) and to ignore the comment. This may work. So can making light of it: "sometimes I don't get it completely right but that just shows people that I'm only human."

If neither of these is effective there are other options, the purpose of which is to let the other person know how you *feel* about the comment.

In put-down situations, using basic assertion as your first response delays the effect you want to achieve, that is, to get the individual to appreciate this comment is hurtful. By immediately asking a question you take the initiative, putting the individual on the back foot.

1. Question assertion A universal response which we have found from experience works in every situation is: It tends to stop people in their tracks; this isn't the reaction they wanted; you are now in control; it gives you time to think of more effective responses, if needed; and now the other person has to explain him or herself.	*"What makes you say that?"*
2. Empathetic assertion Finishing your statement with a question is useful in put-down situations. Asking the question pays respect to those who are not aware they *are* putting you down or appreciate the *effect* it has on you.	*"I sense a certain anxiety in your voice when you say that. Is everything OK with you?"*
3. Discrepancy assertion If the put-downs still persist: *You refer back to a previous discussion or an implicit agreement between you.*	*"Max, on the one hand you agreed to stop being so sarcastic in the office, on the other hand you're still putting people down. What's happened?"*
4. Negative feelings If it continues: *Feelings are at the heart of put-downs. Max may not know how this affects you and you want to use your feelings productively.*	*"Max, I'm angry that you think you can carry on like this, I feel respect between us becomes much harder. I'd like to stop this, what about you?"*

(Continued)

5. Sanctions assertion If they don't stop: *Demonstrates your commitment to a solution and what you are personally prepared to do to bring about a win-win negotiation.*	*"Max, unless you stop sniping at me and others, I'm not going to give you extra support. I don't want to do that, so what can you do?"*
6. Process level Your emotional sensors indicate that there may be other reasons for Max's behaviour. *Process assertion takes the issue "offline," like a "time out," so "positions" can soften and clarifies if there are any underlying issues that are getting in the way of a solution*	*"Max, you repeatedly snipe at me. Is there a deeper underlying problem between us?"*

Praise the behaviour you want

When the put-downs have ceased, you can work on Max's insecurity and praise him when he's open and constructive with his comments. The change does not happen overnight. You need to be persistent, genuine and specific with your praise.

 ## Time to choose

Now think about a situation of your own and write yourself an action plan based on the following questions:

- What specifically are you going to do?
- When will you start it?
- What might be potential barriers to stop you doing it?
- What aspects of this book can help you most in overcoming potential barriers?
- Whose help do you need to support you?
- How will you reward yourself?

6

Getting the Best Out of People at Work

Giving praise and criticism, communicating clearly and getting your requests met

A real-life story

Yt ou have recently been promoted and have taken over the running of an existing customer service team.

You are going to have your first performance review with Phil, the longest serving member of the team and the team leader. You're dreading this meeting because you now have to deliver feedback, which previous managers have been afraid to give to Phil. You know Phil doesn't warm to negative comments about his behaviour and you think he may become unpleasant and throw a tantrum. The thought of the meeting weighs heavy on your mind.

You know Phil to be a hardworking and committed individual. He is detail conscious and meticulous in everything he does. He expects colleagues and customers to know what they want and be clear with him. He is invariably correct in what he says and knows the company's products and services intimately. He is quick and efficient and, on a good day, a mine of knowledge and the go-to person if anyone is unsure about anything.

What causes you significant problems is his downbeat demeanour, his negative attitude towards change and anything new. He has an aggressive, patronizing way when he speaks to colleagues. He struggles to communicate with customers and so comes across as rude and unhelpful. Consistent feedback from customers indicates he lacks empathy and flexibility and some avoid dealing with him. This puts extra strain on other members of your team and is having a negative impact on sales.

The time has come to see if either Phil can change his behaviour or you have to start a disciplinary process that may lead to the termination of his contract.

Wake-up call

Is this happening more and more frequently?

- Customer complaints are on the increase.
- You avoid opportunities to find the time to speak to Phil.
- There's increasing distrust between you and the team.
- More arguments leading to a stifling work environment.
- Team members are avoiding responsibility.
- Morale within the team is suffering.
- Individuals are less flexible over hours and rotas.
- Revenue is suffering.

Standing in the other person's shoes

What might Phil be saying to himself?

- "I do a good job. No one in management has ever said that I don't, or that what I'm doing is wrong."
- "I work hard; do what's asked of me; I'm on time and hardly ever sick, which is a lot more then I can say for some people round here. What more do they want?"
- "I call a spade a spade and don't pander to the customer's whims – half of them don't know what they want a lot of the time."
- "I do things by the book – that's what it's there for – I don't bend the rules."
- "Things have changed; it's not good enough to just do your job you have to be pleasant and mealy mouthed as well."
- "I am who I am and I'm too old to change."

What might other team members be saying to themselves?

- "It's OK for Phil – it seems he can do just as he pleases."
- "If he can get away with it so can we."
- "It's about time management treated us all equally."

- "Customer relationships are not all that important otherwise someone would have spoken to Phil."
- "Perhaps we should behave like him."
- "It's unfair we take on more because customers would rather speak to us than Phil."
- "It's better to avoid Phil when he's in one of his moods."

What might customers be saying to themselves?

- "It's a pain dealing with Phil, it's easier to deal with someone else."
- "You get better service down the road; I don't feel valued."
- "You get good service from other team members; their management must be weak for Phil to get away with it."
- "Courtesy doesn't cost anything; they clearly don't want my business."
- "What kind of company pays for a customer service manager when there is no customer service?"

Taking things on when they're small

What in the past have you allowed to happen? Does any of this sound familiar?

- You've always hated any kind of upset amongst the people you work with and have sought to avoid conflict at all costs.
- You've ignored the first rumblings of discontent amongst the team and hoped things would just improve.
- You've rationalized the increase in complaints as a result of the change in discounts/credit terms for many customers.
- You've justified the fall in revenue on other "technical" issues and a growing competitive market.
- You've hoped morale would magically improve.
- You've rationalized Phil's behaviour is generally OK as everyone has their bad days.
- You've reassured yourself it's not your fault – for years Phil's quirky behaviour has been tolerated.

Options

What mindset would be helpful?

- "I can be firm but fair in my dealings with Phil this afternoon."
- "I can take time now to prepare and make some notes that I can refer to during the review."
- "I can explain the specific behaviours he needs to change and give him examples."
- "I can explain the consequences of his behaviour on customers, myself and the rest of the team."
- "I can praise the specific behaviours that are commendable and again give him examples."
- "I can ask him how he feels about the feedback and show that I've listened."
- "I can give him the opportunity to make the changes needed."
- "I can ask what help he needs from me and the rest of the team."
- "I can explain what will happen if he doesn't change."
- "I can communicate to the whole team the standards of performance I expect."

What permission do you need to give yourself to tackle these situations assertively?

- I have the right to give feedback.
- I have the right to certain standards of performance and behaviour.
- I have the right to develop the skills of my staff.
- I have the right to be open and honest so their careers don't suffer.
- I have the right that my staff should be treated equally.
- I have the right to a response.
- I have the right to be respected.
- I have the right to provide customers with an excellent service.

What win-win outcomes are possible?

- Company revenue targets are met: staff have a job now and in the future.
- I give constructive feedback to Phil: Phil is given the chance to respond and make necessary changes.
- The customer gets the high quality service they deserve: complaints are reduced.
- I'm seen to change inappropriate and dysfunctional behaviour: the team sees we practise what we preach.
- I'm seen to manage difficult situations: an environment of mutual respect is created.

 ## Actions

Prepare your feedback praise and criticism

Research studies on the effects of giving feedback have demonstrated that performance after the interaction is likely to get worse on those aspects of the work on which the job holder has been most severely criticized.

Similar studies have shown that feedback in the form of praise is usually regarded as mere politeness.

Does this mean that giving feedback is a waste of time? Or is there something wrong with the way praise and criticism is actually given? Both practical research and experience support the latter. Many managers in large organizations are crying out for feedback: "tell me what I can do to improve" "tell me how I'm getting on." Skillful feedback is known to improve performance.

Praise

Negative feedback is much more common than positive feedback – praise.

One way to change the culture in an organization is to redress the balance in favour of praise.

Whatever you reward, praise or acknowledge you are likely to get the behaviour you're praising, repeated, i.e. if you want your staff to maintain the levels of performance or go beyond them you need to praise the behaviours they do well.

Around 95% of what your staff do, they do well. Ignore praising them and you seriously run the risk of that percentage diminishing.

Praise works best when it is given close in time to the event.

If you have to give, as in the real-life story at the beginning of this chapter, praise and criticism together – *decouple* them from each other so that they can be *both* valued and heard. And spend equal time on each.

1. Basic assertion *A statement of where you stand, your needs and wants.* This is an example of introducing praise and criticism together and then dealing with them both separately. First we want to concentrate on strengths.	"Phil, I want to discuss a number of things with you about the job. There are many parts you do extremely well and I want to spend some time talking about these. There are some aspects of the job I think we need to look at doing differently and we'll talk about these as well." "First, let's talk about your strengths and the aspects of the job which I think you do well." "Phil, one of your strengths is your attention to detail. For instance, I can always rely on your weekly reports and what I find particularly helpful is the way you lay out the weekly figures." "I am able to understand instantly the key points I need to concentrate on to meet target and I've used your reports with other people to show them how it can be done."

Phil resists . . .	*"It's no big deal, it's something I've always done."*
For some there may be resistance and dismissal of positive feedback because it may be uncomfortable. In Phil's case we imagine there is some resistance if only because he may see it as manipulation and/or sweetening the pill for what is to come later.	

2. Question assertion *Encouraging and inviting a response from others.*	"It takes a lot of sifting through unimportant and important data. How do you do that and get it correct each time?"
Phil resists . . . However spending time discussing their positive behaviour, helps validate the authenticity of your approach.	*"I dunno, it's something I've always been able to do – it's no big deal".*

3. Empathy and questions assertion *Conveys recognition that you understand how others feel.*	"Maybe so. Nevertheless, it's an impressive skill. Would you think about how you do it and would you be prepared to coach others in the team?"
Resistance	*"Um I'm not sure, it would be extra work and I'm already too busy,"*
Response	"I accept that. If we can get other team members to be as accurate as you, we'd save a lot of time overall. I'll work with you to schedule time so you wouldn't have extra work. I'd like this to happen, what do you think?"

Praise the behaviour you want

Manage by walking about so that you can find instances where Phil is either succeeding at the changes he has taken on, or give praise for his honest attempts to do so. Spotting this early reinforces the behavioural changes you both want, and allows you to give any further help if Phil needs it.

Criticism works best when it is specific, i.e. ask yourself what is Phil *doing* or *not doing* that causes a problem and what is the *effect* on *me* and *others*?

Assertive criticism works best when the focus is on the future and what can be done to alter it, not when it is a lengthy post mortem of the past. The past may offer lessons for improvement but you cannot change it.

Clarify your expectations

Beforehand

Ask yourself:

- What is it that the person is doing/or not doing that is causing a problem?
- What is the effect on you/others/the business?

During the feedback

1. Basic assertion

A statement of where you stand, your needs and wants

This is an example of introducing praise and criticism together. Having spent a fulsome amount of time on strengths, we now turn to what we want Phil to change.

"Phil, I now want to talk to you about a couple of aspects of your behaviour where I need you to make a change.

"The first area is to do with communication with colleagues and staff and with customers. There seems to be a similar pattern with all three, so, let me give you an example:

"When you interrupt clients and don't let them finish, they feel their comments are being dismissed and they get angry."

2. Questions Assertion:

Encouraging and inviting a response from others

Question assertion is particularly useful with criticism where you want to:

- Keep defence mechanisms down and minimize resistance to change.
- Allow people to come to their own conclusions about what they do well, not so well, and what they would do differently.
- Give the other person the opportunity for them to give their version. You may have got it wrong or not taken particular circumstances into consideration.

Response from Phil . . .

"What's your view on this?"

"I don't have time to listen to them rambling on, I know what they need even if they don't."

(Continued)

3. Empathy and verbal handshake *Conveys recognition that you understand how others feel. The verbal handshake is a way of getting agreement before going on to solve an issue*	"I can see that you find it frustrating when customers take up a lot of your time because they're unclear. "Phil can you see the problems caused because the customer feels they're being ignored?"
Phil resists . . .	*"Yes, but if I spent a long time talking to all of them I'd never get anything done."*
4. Discrepancy assertion	"We say we believe in listening to our customers but that behaviour shows that we're not interested in their views. "You need to show our customers that we are listening and you need to be a role model for your team."
Phil resists . . .	*"No one's ever criticized the way I deal with customers before and I've been here for some years!"*
5. Negative feelings assertion	"Phil, when you dismiss what people say, it creates resentment and as a result customers are going elsewhere. "I'm disappointed that you sometimes choose to treat customers this way. "In future I'd like you to listen respectfully to every customer."
Phil resists . . .	*"That's all right for you to say, you're not being hassled every day!"*

6. Sanctions assertion	"Phil, this behaviour threatens your career. Unless you can resolve it now you limit your potential with the company.
	"I don't want that to happen so please start behaving more respectfully towards customers from now on.
	"So, specifically, I'd like you to acknowledge them by summarizing what you hear and check you've understood them, before saying what you want to say.
	"How do you feel about this?"
Phil's response . . .	*Looks angry and remains silent*
7. Process assertion	"Phil, are there other issues that you haven't told me about that makes it difficult for you to behave appropriately with customers?"

 ## Time to choose

Now think about a situation of your own and write yourself an action plan based on the following questions:

- What specifically are you going to do?
- When will you start it?
- What might be potential barriers to stop you doing it?
- What aspects of this book can help you most in overcoming potential barriers?
- Whose help do you need to support you?
- How will you reward yourself?

7

Handling Difficult Behaviour and Coping with Conflict

Dealing with aggression and gaining commitment from others

A real-life story

You're an ambitious person who has lots of ideas of how to improve sales, and increase capacity within the company you have just joined. At your interview you were told that you got the job because you were very direct, enthusiastic and had lots of ideas.

Since starting the job, it's always been clear to you that there are vast areas of the business that could be improved without incurring any significant costs. Your enthusiasm for bringing them about, however, has waned during the year you've been there.

At the beginning, your ideas were acknowledged and even welcomed by senior managers. The reality one year later, however, is different. Your immediate boss Sally, whilst clearly competent, has been dismissive over your suggestions to increase capacity. She has also seemed quite resistant towards your ideas, saying things like: "they won't like it, that won't work we've tried that before."

As a result, you do not see eye to eye with Sally, and so, in terms of influence, you have quite a challenge. Sally sees you as a threat to her control, and what she sees as her responsibility to initiate and manage change.

Her own boss Mike is younger and very clever, but less experienced and leans on Sally for guidance.

Recently, Mike asked what you'd do to improve team working in his department. You discuss this with your team and present some proposals to Mike. You realize though that Mike tends to avoid making any decisions and is perhaps just going through the motions of what a good boss is "supposed" to do.

Mike is capable of many things but facing up to conflict is not one of them. His response to conflict is to say something authoritative using "management speak" and then quickly walk away leaving you no chance to reply.

At the same time, Sally sees this as you manipulating the situation to usurp her authority and undermine her position. Sally has called you in for a "clear the air" conversation. You suspect that this could develop into a heated debate.

Wake-up call

Is this happening more and more frequently?

- You've invested too much of your ego in your ideas i.e. a rejection of your ideas is a rejection of you.
- You've given in easily if an idea you put forward is dismissed.
- You're not as confident in your ideas as you were.
- You're not so positive about yourself in your ability to change things.
- You are less prepared to challenge.
- You don't follow up on any of your suggestions, you just let them be ignored.
- You're more tolerant of inefficiencies.

Standing in the other person's shoes

What might Sally be saying to herself?

- "Who do they think they are?"
- "They're just trying to cause trouble."
- "Do they want my job?"
- "Before they stuck their nose in, everything was just ticking along nicely."
- "I know what works, and what doesn't; they've only been here a short time."
- "We need stability not constant change."

- "I should be seen as the innovator, not them."
- "Any changes might reduce the control I have."

What might Mike be saying to himself?

- "I need to be seen as interested in continuous improvement."
- "I can ask for ideas but don't have to do anything about them."
- "I can say 'I'll think about it'."
- "I wish the two of them could get on better."
- "No need to be too hasty, things always sort themselves out in the end."

Taking things on when they're small

What in the past have you allowed to happen? Does any of this sound familiar?

- You've made suggestions without asking for Sally's views.
- You've put ideas in writing presenting them as a *fait accompli*.
- Your suggestions haven't taken into consideration the culture of the company – you've pushed for revolution rather than evolution the limitations.
- You've been quick to point out limitations of Sally's suggestions.
- You've made Mike the "piggy in the middle" with some of your altercations with Sally.
- You've pushed Mike hard for decisions instead of looking for alternative ways round problems.

Options

What mindset would be helpful with Mike?

- "I can involve Sally more in the build-up to suggestions and proposals."

- "I can be more selective about which changes will have the greatest impacts and put those rather than all my ideas forward."
- "I can be more sensitive to some of the resistors to change and use Mike and Sally as sounding boards."
- "I can still put my suggestions forward with enthusiasm but not see rejection of them as rejection of me and my ability."
- "I can find more creative ways to present suggestions."
- "I can separate what I think are 'good' ideas from the 'bad' ideas in Sally's suggestions and acknowledge the good."
- "In the spirit of learning I can find out from Mike and Sally what my previous suggestions lacked."

What mindset would be helpful to Sally?

- "I can stand my ground respectfully when facing conflict."
- "I can apply the techniques that will keep me grounded, respectful and assertive if the conversation becomes heated."
- "I can maintain my assertion and handle any aggression by being calm and in control of myself and my emotions."
- "I can maintain my assertion and encourage Sally to be assertive."
- "I can strive for an outcome that is good for both of us."

What permission do you need to give yourself to tackle these situations assertively?

- I have the right to look for ways of improving business and business processes.
- I have the right to put forward ideas I think would benefit the company.
- I have the right to get a response to those ideas.
- I have a right to receive feedback and learn from others' suggestions.
- I have a right to be treated with respect.

What win-win outcomes are possible?

- I put my ideas forward sensitively: others are more ready to accept them.
- I listen to their concerns: they feel more acknowledged and heard.
- We work more as a team: Sally and Mike feel more in control.
- Greater cohesion amongst staff: more willingness to strive for better results.
- Higher expectations set: sales and capacity are increased.

Actions

Handling a difficult conversation with Mike

This could be a situation where it's difficult to get commitment from someone. To understand their views, thoughts and concerns becomes a struggle because their behaviour can either be non-assertive or passive aggressive. More generally, they're reluctant to give a decision or will issue a command and provide no explanation.

In the example below, you've tried on a number of occasions to get Mike's attention to discuss various ideas you have. Each time he has made some excuse, but today you have managed to engage him.

1. Basic assertion *You put your view forward.*	"Mike you wanted some ideas from me about how we can improve teamwork and here they are."
Mike resists . . .	*"Leave them with me, I probably won't have a chance to look at them for the next few weeks because I'm so busy, sorry."*

(Continued)

161

2. Question assertion *You ask his view.*	"Have you just ten minutes to discuss the main points?"
Mike resists...	*"Well I'd rather have a chance to read them through first and then speak to you."*
3. Empathy assertion *You acknowledge his view and move the discussion forward.*	"I know how busy you are and I don't expect you to make any decisions now, I'd still like to highlight one or two of the main points to see if I'm on the right track."
Mike resists...	*Sighs... "Ok but you'll have to be quick, you've got a couple of minutes."*
4. Discrepancy assertion *You point out the gap between what is being said and what is being done.*	"Mike, last week you told me you wanted ideas to improve teamwork as soon as possible. Now you're saying you don't have time to discuss them. When can we make time?"
Mike resists...	*"I'm sorry but I can't make any decisions without involving others."*
5. Negative feelings assertion You describe the negative impact of his behaviour on you/others/the business.	"When you delay our discussions I feel frustrated. "It's affecting my morale and others in the team because we don't get any response to our proposals. "When can we make some time in your diary?"
Mike resists...	*"Look, I feel you're pressuring me. I've told you I will give you an answer later. I've got to go now."*
6. Sanctions assertion	"Unless we get feedback to our ideas I feel sure that the team in the future are going to be reluctant to generate any. "So when are you available to discuss these?"
Mike resists...	*Looks angry and remains silent*
7. Process assertion	"Mike, are there other issues that you've not mentioned that make it difficult for you to listen to our ideas?"

4Ps and aggression

When someone is acting aggressively, normally it is because they have lost control – over themselves or the situation – they feel only by shouting louder and being angry will anything will be done, e.g. "It's only when I get angry that you listen . . ." Aggression needs an aggressive reaction to sustain its momentum.

The 4P approach aims first to give you control and remove the heat from the situation and, second, to calm the other person so that they are able to solve the problem by methods other than being aggressive. It also encourages people to think.

1. **Pause.** Be prepared to listen and indicate that is what you are doing. Let the other person "empty."
2. **Probe.**
   Open questions make the person think and helps them engage their brain. Open questions will also help you identify the real problem.
   Test your understanding of their problem, this will help to show you care and have listened.
   Listen for the clues – to ask further questions – they are always there!
3. **Posture.** Although you cannot always be seen (over the telephone) you need to create a firm posture in the way you are sitting or standing. You need to sense the strength of your own body and let this strength transmit itself through your voice.
4. **Pace.** Reduce the speed at which you might normally speak and engage the person in a firm but caring tone. Empathize with their position and, once you have understood it, indicate what you will do next.
   When the appropriate level of empathy has been established – "lead the individual" into solving the problem.

Handling a conflict situation with Sally

In the example below you are having a "clear the air" conversation with Sally which initially seemed to be going ok but you sense a growing frustration from Sally towards you.

You make a suggestion to which Sally responds aggressively.

Posture	Throughout the interaction be aware of demonstrating an open posture, upright and "earthed." Your face needs to be equally open as do any hand gestures you make.
Pace	Throughout the interaction be aware of slowing down the speed at which you talk. When you ask the questions, slow it down and emphasize action words rather than nouns and pronouns.
Sally's aggression	*"I don't think you're in a position to make suggestions like these – you haven't been here long enough, it's always worked for us in the past . . ."*
Pause	You remain silent, don't interrupt, acknowledge what she's saying non-verbally and allow Sally to finish.
Probe Question assertion to understand the specific nature of the issue.	"What specifically is it that you don't like about my proposals?"
Sally's aggression	*"It's always the same: you think you know best, you just can't accept that things worked perfectly well before you ever arrived, you just want to cause trouble in order to get recognition . . ."*
Pause	To allow Sally to finish

Probe Empathy & Question assertion to get to the route of the problem and not get diverted by other issues	"I sense you feel strongly about this, what is it that I've proposed that you don't like?"
Sally's aggression continues	*"I just don't trust your motives, we have to work as a team, you can't just go off on your own all the time as if I wasn't involved."*
Pause	So we show we've listened to what Sally has said
Probe Empathy and question assertion to get to the route of the problem	"I can see that we have a different way of approaching things. I certainly meant no disrespect. "Are there any other objections you have to my proposals?"
Sally's aggression	*"Now you come to mention it . . . I feel undermined when you don't consult me on these proposed changes. I do have a view about them yet you don't consult me but go straight to Mike. I could help because I know the system and could point you in the right direction so that it would have greater impact with Mike. I feel like you don't respect my position."*
Pause	To again show we've listened to what Sally has said

(Continued)

Probe	"I hadn't appreciated I'd had that effect. I very much want to work as a team and welcome your input. What do we need to do to ensure we work better together in the future?"
Sally's emotional release	*"So you realize you do need my help now.* *"Well it's just a shame you didn't see that in the first place!"*
Probe *Questions assertion*	"I always want your help, so can we discuss now what you think I need to do now in relation to the team building proposal. Can we talk about it now?"
An assertive discussion takes place.	

 ## Time to choose

Now think about a situation of your own and write yourself an action plan based on the following questions:

- What specifically are you going to do?
- When will you start it?
- What might be potential barriers to stop you doing it?
- What aspects of this book can help you most in overcoming potential barriers?
- Whose help do you need to support you?
- How will you reward yourself?

8

Being Assertive in Meetings and Presentations

Getting our views heard and getting our butterflies under control

A real-life story

Your team has been consistently the number one performer against all key performance indicators – from revenue earning, to customer satisfaction, to service delivery. You know you're highly respected by your team. You're a good leader and coach. Last year when an internal vacancy arose it was an easy decision for the company to promote you to the position of area manager.

As expected, your area now outperforms all others and further promotion beckons.

There is, however, one significant "fly in the ointment." At first it was something you were prepared to live with but, with each passing month, it has become a serious roadblock to your promotion.

Every quarter, the company holds a regional meeting where area managers, regional managers and senior staff conduct a strategic review of the direction of the company. Everyone is expected to participate in decisions that affect the ongoing strategic plan. In addition to these regional meetings, area managers meet every six weeks to decide on more tactical issues.

In both types of meetings you're expected to make a presentation on your operation and take a vigorous part in a two-day discussion. You find it easier to make presentations to your staff but, when it comes to presenting in front of your peers and senior management, you rush through the presentation and dread the moment when you have to answer questions. Despite wanting to, your contribution to discussions is almost entirely absent and you never ask any questions.

Before a recent regional meeting you had asked one of your fellow area managers, Linda, to take the lead on a very contentious issue and when she looked to you for support you remained silent.

You're told by your boss that others now interpret your lack of involvement as arrogance. You're told that your peers and senior management are losing patience with you and seriously doubt whether you should attend these meetings at all, as your behaviour is having a negative impact on them.

You're losing credibility and respect and you can hardly expect further promotion, as the next logical move would be national operations manager, managing all the area managers.

You want to present and be a fully active team member. You also still want to progress further in the company so now is the time to act.

 ## Wake-up call

Is this happening more and more frequently?

- You find it difficult to sleep prior to the meetings and generally lose your appetite.
- You've that sinking feeling in your stomach every time you think about them.
- Other work duties suffer as you lose focus and attention.
- You're short-tempered with people.
- You constantly rehearse in your head how you are going to fail.
- You seriously doubt your ability ever to be able to cope, and start believing this is the way it will always be.
- You avoid meetings where there may be a significant number of people you don't know.
- You're getting really frustrated with yourself – you've had enough.

Standing in the other person's shoes

What might others be saying about your behaviour?

- "I wish you'd realize, we want to hear your views and ideas."
- "You've a lot to contribute – what's holding you back?"
- "We understand you're shy but, at your age, you should be able to get over it."
- "Are we that difficult to talk to or do you think you're just superior to us?"
- "If you are not contributing what are you doing here?"
- "Do you agree, disagree or just can't be bothered to comment?"
- "We listen and comment on your presentation – is it too much to ask you do the same for ours?"
- "Are you committed? Can you be bothered to make this group a success?"

Taking things on when they're small

What in the past have you allowed to happen? Does any of this sound familiar?

- You've never sought feedback on your presentations.
- You've never received enthusiastic feedback so you think you're boring.
- You've not prepared your presentations with your audience in mind – you believe you know what they need to know.
- You've allowed meetings to ramble on without making any interventions or challenges.
- You think you know what others are going to say – so stop listening and switch off.
- You don't join in the social element at team functions.
- You gravitate towards only people you know and avoided "strangers."

- You feel you never know what to say to start a conversation and so don't try.
- You find it hard to disclose anything personal about yourself.
- You can't find the energy to make the effort to make new relationships.

 Options

What mindset would be helpful?

- "Even if there are people there who I don't know, I don't need to be overwhelmed, I can stay calm."
- "When it's my turn to present, no need for hysterics, keep it low key."
- "If I don't know the answer to something, I can say I'll get back to them, I don't need to know everything."
- "Beforehand, I can ask others what they want me to include in my presentation so that I don't waste valuable airtime."
- "Meetings are not a combat zone but a means of finding out information and ideas."
- "I can't be certain that I know what others are thinking, I can show interest and ask."
- "I can be more spontaneous without having to think things through first. I don't need to be word perfect."
- "My ideas count and I've a responsibility to help these meetings along."
- "It'll be a challenge but I can reveal something about myself to others and ask them about their kids/weekend etc."

What permission do you need to give yourself to tackle these situations assertively?

- I have the right to change things about myself I don't like.
- I have the right to be human i.e. to make a mistake, or not to know something.

- I have the right to be different from others.
- I have the right to contribute my thoughts and ideas.
- I have the right to a fair hearing for these.
- I have the right to be treated equally and with respect.
- I have the right to feedback.
- I have the right to use my time effectively and do the best I can for my operation.

What win-win outcomes are possible?

- Others find out where you stand on issues: you will become more involved in meetings.
- Others feel you are part of the team: building relationships is easier.
- Others feel listened to: the company has better informed decisions.
- Your self-confidence increases: meetings are better organized and focused.
- The company has a more responsible manager: your career development is still open.
- Reduced stress and anxiety in your life: greater productivity and performance for the company.

 Actions

Normally it is easier to build rapport and have a deeper meaningful conversation with one person than two and even harder with three, four, etc.

It is harder in these situations for you to judge whether people are interested or not, bored or enthralled by what you are saying. You become uncertain, hesitant and prone to ramble as you search for some flicker of interest from others.

You find it more difficult to get feedback, you may feel judged and under greater pressure to perform.

The way out of this dilemma for you is to keep quiet and maintain a low profile till in the end you may withdraw more from the meeting.

The likelihood is you may want to contribute but leave it later and later till you do. Consequently, what would have been quite simple and easy now becomes a difficult challenge. Here are some ways of managing your fears when participating in meetings and making presentations.

Participating in meetings

1. Enter early
The earlier you can say something, the better it is – breaking the ice early is important and, because it is at the beginning, needn't be profound. A simple answer to a question delivered with a modicum of gusto will suffice, "I agree with that" or "have we all read the minutes" or "I hope we are all looking forward to having a good meeting" will go a long way and gives you early entry.

If there are a number of presentations being made at the meeting, ask if you can make the *first* presentation so you have already been a part of the meeting and are more likely to continue your participation.

2. Practise assertive active listening
Whether you say anything or not at a meeting, you can participate significantly and make a considerable difference to the atmosphere and climate of the meeting by assertive active listening, "So what I've heard you say is that you're concerned about the status and you want suggestions for change." Feedback at meetings is, as we

have said, generally "low" and anyone who actively listens encourages the speaker. You have at least one ally!

3. Signal your intention

Imagine you are driving a car in busy traffic and want to turn left or right, you increase your chances to be able to do so if you signal your intention before actually turning left or right. Other drivers will allow you to enter into their space.

Signalling is a communication technique that does exactly the same thing. Signal what you are going to say and then say it. The signal part of the message can be made stronger than what you're actually going to say and thus get attention without seeming aggressive, rude or loud. For example:

> "*I'd like to make an observation* . . . can we look at the parking fees first before we move on?"
>
> "*I'd like to add* . . . I think we should increase the allowance for staff."
>
> "*I would like to clarify what John just said* . . . are we going to ask for voluntary contributions from staff?"
>
> "*So to summarize* . . . we've agreed Cedric and Bella will be our representatives."
>
> "*Can I ask a question* . . . when are we going to decide on the launch date?"

4. Choose where you sit

Where you sit is important. You need to be in a position where you can catch the eye of most people and, particularly, the chair person. You may be reticent to participate, so avoid taking the opt-out option at the ends of the table.

Position your chair so that you are sitting as close to the table as everyone else. You will signify non-verbally that you are not a part of the meeting if you draw your chair back farther than anyone else.

5. Work on your body language

When you do want to enter and speak in the meeting make a change in your body posture, leaning forward. Movement signals that something different is going to happen and will be picked up directly as well as peripherally.

In addition, there are six specific behaviours, which can help you contribute assertively to a meeting.

1. State your views Clearly and concisely.	*"In my view ..."* *"I suggest that ..."* *"As I see it ..."*
2. Support Let people know what you agree with. Supporting creates a creative and win-win atmosphere.	*"I think that's a good idea."* *"I agree with Jon's idea."*
3. Propose and suggest These are the behaviours that bring about action and movement in a meeting. The lack of these behaviours causes the conversation to go round and round and round ...	*"I'd like to suggest that ..."* *"How about we take action now?"*
4. State differences Differences can lead to a better result. So air them and keep them in proportion.	*"I see it differently because ..."* *"I agree with that last point, and have some doubts about ..."*

5. Ask for clarification The only dumb question is the question you don't ask.	*"What's your view on . . .?"* *"How does that fit into what we've agreed?"* *"When you said you were concerned, what were you thinking of?"*
6. Summarize Frequent summaries allow decisions and action to be understood and lend clarity to what has been said.	*"I'd like to check what we've agreed so far."* *"Can we summarize where we are?"*

Try one behaviour at a time – become competent at it and then choose another until you have all six in your repertoire.

Making presentations

1. Beforehand
Presentations normally have a degree of self-induced stress. The bottom line is, "will you look a fool?"

When you put all your attention on your survival, most of your energy is directed inwards. When you put your attention on the message the energy is directed outwards, where it serves you best.

Always know the outcome you want from a presentation. Ask yourself some questions to clarify your outcome before the presentation.

- "What is the key message you are putting across?" Summarize it in one sentence.
- "What are the benefits to your audience?"
- "Are there any natural allies or potential opposition in the group you are presenting to?"

- "Do you have all the facts you need for this presentation?"
- "What are the most difficult questions that you could be asked?"

If you find presentations particularly fear-inducing, you can reduce your fear of uncertainty by asking a few colleagues if you can present to them and brief them to ask the most difficult questions.

2. During

Make your first outcome to gain rapport with the audience. This is very simple: get them to share some experience as a group. Otherwise refer to some shared experience – the journey, the weather, it doesn't matter what.

Second, establish your credibility. Introduce yourself briefly, say who invited you to present or give any other appropriate referrals.

Third, establish a mood of acceptance right from the start. You can do this with quite mundane remarks or with rhetorical questions. "We are all here, aren't we?" "The projector is plugged in, isn't it?" "Can we open a window – it's a bit stuffy in here, isn't it?"

Don't underestimate the power of the obvious, because it is powerful.

Fourthly, set out the way you plan the presentation right from the start. There is a lot of truth in the saying, "Tell them what you are going to tell them, tell them, then tell them what you have told them."

Make *KISS* you motto: **Keep It Short and Simple.** Very few people remember more than *five points* from a presentation anyway. Decide in advance which five you want them to remember. People have the greatest recall of what was said in the first few minutes and the last few minutes, so make the key points there.

Praise the behaviour you want

Whatever happens in the presentation or in the meeting, learn from it afterwards. When you've finished, congratulate yourself and ask, "How might I have done better?"

Give yourself permission to make mistakes, the best in every field do.

Reward yourself for the efforts you made, for taking a risk and going beyond your comfort zone, whether you're completely successful or not. The longest journey starts with the first step.

 ## Time to choose

Now think about a situation of your own and write yourself an action plan based on the following questions:

- What specifically are you going to do?
- When will you start it?
- What might be potential barriers to stop you doing it?
- What aspects of this book can help you most in overcoming potential barriers?
- Whose help do you need to support you?
- How will you reward yourself?

9
Families – Who'd Have 'em?

Managing kids, handling teenagers and coping with partners and parents assertively

A real-life story

You arrive home after a hard day at the office to find clothes, shoes and sports bags scattered about the hallway.

Dirty plates and mugs are strewn around the kitchen.

The washing is still sat in the machine and nobody's thought to peel some vegetables for dinner.

The TV drones on whilst a fight for the remote ensues in the background. There's a message from Social Services to say your mother's personal alarm, that she wears in case she has another fall, has been going off continually today because she keeps triggering it by mistake.

There's a message from your mum fretting about renewing her house insurance and asking if you could sort it straight away.

Your partner has texted you to say they'll be home late and would you apologize on their behalf to the PTA, for their absence at this evening's meeting.

You put your bags down and slump into the only chair that's free of debris. You ask yourself, "why do I have to do everything? How would they cope if I wasn't here? Why can't people take responsibility for their actions?"

Does any of this sound familiar?

Wake-up call

Is this happening more and more frequently?

- You're becoming increasingly tired because you're doing everything.

- You're feeling more put upon and taken for granted.
- Even the more simple things aren't being done.
- You're angry from the moment you come in.
- You either suppress your anger or you lose your temper at the smallest thing.
- You say to yourself "I don't know how much longer this can continue."

Standing in the other person's shoes

What might other members of the family be saying to themselves?

- "I'm doing what I want to do."
- "I can't be bothered, it doesn't concern me, it's not my job."
- "I'm doing something, *that* can wait till later on."
- "Why should I think about anybody else's needs, they don't think about me?"
- "If you want it done so badly why don't you do itself?"
- "Others can do what they want, it's up to them."
- "Why should I have to do something I don't enjoy?"
- "I don't want to be a bother so I won't complain about the alarm."
- "How many times do I need to tell them that my house insurance needs sorting?"
- "I haven't got time to get into a lengthy discussion with the PTA chairman, my 'other half' can sort it out."

Taking things on when they're small

What in the past have you allowed to happen? Does any of this sound familiar?

- You haven't kept your promise to impose sanctions if the kids don't tidy up after themselves.

- You're seen as the bad cop while your partner is the one who always "gives in."
- It's been quicker to do the vegetables yourself than to argue about it.
- When someone has lost something like their sports kit you're the one that goes looking for it.
- You haven't taken the time to remind your mother about what to do when she triggers the alarm by mistake.
- You've kept putting off sorting out your mum's insurance.
- You haven't told other members of your mum's family that you need help.
- You haven't calmly sat down with your partner and been honest with them, about how you allow their behaviour to affect you and the pressure it puts you under – instead, you've lost your temper.
- You hint at wanting to be helped but don't directly ask your partner.
- You don't want to ask for help because it looks like you can't cope.

 ## Options

What mindset would be helpful?

- "I don't have to let things continue as they are. I can talk to everyone calmly about my expectations and I can ask them about theirs."
- "I don't have to tackle everything at once I can start with something small and build on it."
- "A good parent is someone who encourages children to grow up responsibly."
- "If I aim to be fair and reasonable I can encourage others to co-operate."
- "Being firm, fair and consistent will get more respect from young people."

- "Making young people 'responsible' prepares them for life."
- "I can explain to mum the consequences of her alarm going off unnecessarily."
- "I'll diarize key dates when things need renewing for mum."
- "I can ask my partner to agree to a more equitable share of family and household responsibilities."

What permission do you need to give yourself to tackle these situations assertively?

- I have the right to be helped.
- I have the right to be a helper not a doer.
- I have the right to agree expectations and have them met.
- I have the right to develop the children's life skills.
- I have the right to have a well-balanced life.
- I have the right to only take on an equal share of responsibilities.

What win-win outcomes are possible?

- My kids can grow up to be more independent and better prepared for life: I can take some credit for that.
- My mother's situation is considered more: our lives are less stressful.
- The children aren't nagged over small matters: I lose my temper less.
- Work is more equitably shared: I feel more valued and a "whole" person.
- We have more "quality" time as a family.

 Actions

Listening

Domestic situations like these can be emotional, especially if you have not done anything about them before. The temptation would either be, to challenge people non-assertively, not wanting to upset them or cause an argument; or, you may want to hammer home your point and command that they respect your authority.

One of the first things we fail to do is listen. In these situations we need particularly to be conscious of deciding to listen, acknowledge and understand without interrupting.

Clarify your expectations of children
You may decide the first thing you want to tackle might be help with the washing/ironing. Problems often occur in relationships when people have different expectations of each other and these are not clarified. You can clarify the situation by using the ideas in the table below.

1. Basic assertion *A statement of where you stand, your needs and wants.*	"At the moment what's going on doesn't work for me. I'd like everyone to be pulling their weight when they get home and share the household chores, particularly with the washing and ironing." "In future, if you get home before me and there's washing in the machine please hang it up to dry."
2. Question assertion *Encouraging and inviting a response from others.*	"I think that's fair how do you feel about that?"
Your family agree to this:	*"Yeah ok we'll do it."*
Let's imagine you come home again and things haven't changed even though they agreed to co-operate:	

(*Continued*)

3. Empathy assertion *Conveys recognition that you understand how other's feel.*	"I know you've had a long day at school and the match this afternoon was particularly gruelling. I still need your help getting things done."
Let's imagine you come back again and things still haven't changed:	
4. Discrepancy assertion *You refer back to a previous discussion or an implicit agreement between you.*	"We agreed that when you get home you'd hang the washing out if it's not raining. It's sunny and it's still sitting in the machine, so in future I'd like you to do what we agreed."
Let's imagine you still get resistance and things haven't changed:	*"I was going to do it, it doesn't have to be done right this minute!"*
5. Negative feelings assertion *Feelings are an important part of personal influence and can often be the key to show implications on you and how you feel about them.*	"We've had a number of conversations and you did agree to help out, this hasn't happened because when I get home I find you sitting in front of the TV and the washing's still in the machine. I feel angry. What do we need to do to make sure this happens?"
Let's imagine you still get resistance and things haven't changed:	*"It's not fair. My friends' parents don't make them do housework when they get home from school."*
6. Sanctions assertion *Demonstrates your commitment to a solution and what you are personally prepared to do to bring about a win-win negotiation.*	"If you refuse to help I'll have to ration the amount of TV until these chores have been done."

Praise the behaviour you want

When the kids do what you ask, acknowledge it and give praise and let them know how it has helped.

"James, thanks for hanging the washing out, it meant that I could get on with the dinner so that we didn't have to gulp our food down before we went to cricket practice tonight."

Building on success

Consistently catch your children doing "good' things. Give short (more play time, some extra TV time etc.), as well as longer term rewards (trips out, gifts, etc.), and also verbal praise to grow their self-esteem and confidence.

Clarify your expectations of your partner

Again problems occur between couples because you assume that your partner should know what you want and you get frustrated and angry when they seem oblivious.

The situation below makes the assumption that this request to cancel the PTA is symptomatic of a regular occurrence where you are expected to "drop' everything and react to your partner's request as an immediate priority.

You can clarify the situation by using the ideas in the table below.

Basic assertion	"I think you need to cancel the PTA meeting."
Resistance . . .	*"But it would only take you a moment."*
Question assertion	"It may do. What stops you telephoning them yourself?"
resistance	*"I am very busy at the moment, can't you do it for me, just this time?"*

(Continued)

Empathy assertion	"I know you have a lot on and I would like to finish what I am doing. I prefer it if you make the call this time."
Resistance...	*"We're spending longer on which one of us is going to make it than it would take, to actually make the call. Surely, it's easier for you than me?"*
Negative feelings assertion	"When you're not mindful of things I have to do and expect me to drop everything, I get angry. I feel you don't respect that I've things to do as well. This is an example of that and I believe you should make the call."
Resistance...	*"Oh, I think that's unfair – all I want you to do for me is to make a thirty second call!"*
Consequences assertion	"I need you to be more respectful of my time and unless you are, I can see myself being constantly irritated and snappy with you. I don't want to be like that so I'd like you to make the call instead."
Resistance...	*"It really won't take you long."*
Process	"No. I really believe you need to do it. When we have a quiet moment later can we talk about how we help and don't help each other out generally?"

Praise the behaviour you want

When your partner does cooperate in the way you had hoped, acknowledge it and give praise and let them know how it has helped.

"I appreciate you sharing the responsibility of talking to the kids about the mess etc. and I feel more appreciated by you. The kids seem happier too."

Building on success
Notice the occasions when your partner continues to share the load and express appreciation for them, listen effectively and make further decisions together.

Every time we succeed at being assertive it's evidence of how we're progressing and provides others with proof of how their behaviour can change too.

 ## Time to choose

Now think about a situation of your own and write yourself an action plan based on the following questions:

- What specifically are you going to do?
- When will you start it?
- What might be potential barriers to stop you doing it?
- What aspects of this book can help you most in overcoming potential barriers?
- Whose help do you need to support you?
- How will you reward yourself?

10
Friends, Neighbours and Social Occasions

Managing different expectations and keeping relationships in tact

A real-life story

You get on really well with your three sets of friends/neighbours and their children, which is why you've agreed to go on holiday together. There's always lots of laughter and fun when you meet up socially. The planning and organizing of the trip has been relatively easy and expectations are running high of a good time.

Finding out new things about friends can be fun but you are finding out more than you bargained for. After three days together the relationships are becoming seriously strained. This is largely due to different people having different priorities, interests and expectations about the holiday and who should do what, if anything!

* It was you who picked up the tab for the drinks and sandwiches but there is a continued reluctance for your friends to share equally with expenses.
* Some of you have come away to chill, lie by the pool and read a book, others have come intent to discover the rich history of their surroundings.
* Cooking with the local fresh exotic produce is high on one couple's agenda whilst another desperately seeks to maintain their fitness.
* Your friends don't like their children to stay up too late whereas you're happy that your children go to bed much later.
* You hoped everyone would take turns at cooking and shopping whilst others seem to want to eat out every night.
* You like to clear everything away before you go to bed whilst others are content to wash the dishes when they feel like it.
* You enjoy background music whilst others are content with the sounds of nature.
* You like to plan whilst others prefer spontaneity.

You value your friends and you'd like the holiday to get back on the right footing so you decide to talk to them.

Wake-up call

Is this happening more and more frequently?

- On the one hand, individuals are reluctant to put forward their point of view. On the other hand, sometimes they do so without due consideration for others.
- The atmosphere is getting more tense.
- There are more and more covert non-verbal signals i.e. nods, winks and eyes rolling.
- Little things are upsetting everyone.
- There's a strained politeness creeping in.
- More arguments with the children can be overheard.
- Less laughter than normal.

Standing in the other person's shoes

What might others be saying to themselves?

- "Live and let live."
- "Why didn't we have a plan before we came away?"
- "Nobody seems to care what I want."
- "This is supposed to be a holiday not a conflict zone."
- "Who do they think they are?"
- "It's only two weeks, it's easier to stay quiet."
- "Why is it always me who has to be so tolerant for the sake of maintaining the peace?"
- "We should all be pulling our weight."
- "They don't discipline – they let their children do what they want."
- "They just like complaining."
- "If it wasn't for me, nothing would happen."
- "There'll definitely be a row this time."

Taking things on when they're small

What in the past have you allowed to happen? Does any of this sound familiar?

- You've agreed with others when you'd actually prefer to do something else.
- You've resisted speaking up when you've been unhappy about a decision.
- You've sought to avoid conflict.
- You've let the little niggles grow into big issues.
- You always see both sides of the argument and are reluctant to choose one way or the other.
- You don't want to upset anyone.
- You've let others take responsibility for sorting things out.
- You blame others when things aren't going right rather than look at your part in the dispute.

Options

What mindset would be helpful?

- "These are my friends after all – I should be able to discuss our different expectations."
- "We don't all have to do the same things at the same time."
- "I don't have to agree with everything, I can state my preferences.
- "We all have different expectations and we can talk about them."
- "I'm responsible for my own behaviour, they are for theirs."
- "If there's an awkward exchange I can keep calm."
- "I can give everyone their own space and time."
- "I don't have to get upset by the small things, I can put them into perspective."
- "I'm sure we can set boundaries that all of us are comfortable with."

What permission do you need to give yourself to tackle these situations assertively?

- I have the right to expect that we all take equal responsibility for the success of the holiday.
- I have the right to expect we all pay our fair share of expenses.
- I have the right to be open and honest and clear about what I want.
- I have the right to see where others stand on certain issues.
- I have the right to say I don't have a preference.
- I have the right to be myself (different from what others may expect me to be).
- I have the right to use my time in the way I want to.
- I have the right not to feel I'm being taken advantage of.
- I have the right to enjoy doing the things I want to do.

What win-win outcomes are possible?

- We can be honest with each other: relationships are strengthened not diminished.
- The air is cleared, hidden agendas are out in the open: we trust one another more and feel more at ease.
- We can say what we need to say without feeling guilty: we learn more about one another's preferences.
- Expectations are largely met: we all have the rest and fun we had hoped for.
- We've learnt from this experience: we know how to do this again in the future.

 Actions

A part of your uniqueness is that you have different expectations, neither better nor worse than other people. Disappointment often arises because these expectations are not met and not realistic.

In this instance, we are looking at holidays but it is also true of many social situations involving friends, neighbours and relatives such as weddings, dinner parties, BBQs and funerals.

Holidays are meant to be enjoyable. After all, you have saved hard for a chance to get away from your everyday stresses, and enjoy the things you want to do.

Your expectations play a pivotal part in creating the outcome you have in mind. Holidays that exceed our expectations do happen but you can't always make them perfect, and friends don't always get along.

Sitting down with friends in a relaxed social setting and openly discussing expectations and boundaries will go a long way to ensuring a happier more stress free holiday. It is a prerequisite for clearing the air and setting more realistic expectations that include the hopes and dreams of others.

Include in your discussion all or some of the following:

- your budget – what you intend to spend whilst away;
- eating in or out – sharing of the cooking and shopping;
- children – bed times and activities;
- relaxing or active holiday or both – planning places to visit in advance;
- time and commitment – together all the time and having your own space; and
- housekeeping – sharing the chores.

Work out what you *do* and *don't* want to do and be open about it. It will encourage others to be the same. Be prepared to say "no' to things that you are sure you don't want to do.

Most importantly, know what you can control and what you can't i.e. you are responsible for your own behaviour, feelings and emotions. You cannot control other peoples' attitudes and expectations. Instead of stressing over things, let go of those things you can't control.

You may not have done any of the above, which could be why you now want to have a discussion with the friends you value.

The following example might be a way of approaching a conversation with your friends. Thoughtful planning of what you're going to say beforehand will help you be very specific about things, which makes it easier for people to engage with you and is more likely to avoid the discussion becoming emotional highly charged.

Timing is also a key factor to your success here. Choose a time to discuss things when people seem relaxed and distanced from any specific event that may cause tension.

Use of the verbal handshake will prove valuable here.

1. **Basic and Questions assertion**	"I'm feeling unhappy about some of the things that are going unsaid on this holiday, so can we sit down and have a chat?"
Response from others	*"What's bothering you?"*
2. **Basic and Questions assertion**	"Well, I feel it would be helpful to air our views about expenditure, sharing the cooking and chores, planning some activities in advance so we don't make decisions at the last minute and generally agreeing how we want to be when we're all together."
	"How do the rest of you feel about this?"
Resistance from others	*"This is a holiday not an exercise in project management, we've come away to relax not adhere to some rigorous plan!"*

3. Basic and Questions assertion – and use of the **Verbal sandwich**	"Yes I agree and I appreciate that we've all come away to enjoy ourselves and leave work behind." "Do you agree that over the last couple of days there has been some tension building amongst us?"
Response from others	*"Well now you come to mention it yes."*
4. Basic and Questions assertion	"We're friends and I'd like to think we can talk about things openly. So I'd like to ease that tension, discuss any issues, clear the air. How do the rest of you feel about that?"
Response from others	*"Ok let's get on with it."*
5. Basic and Questions assertion	"So let's list the subjects we want to agree on and share our views as to how we might do this." "These are mine: "Cooking and washing up, paying for things when we're out together and planning collective trips and activities. "What do you want to add?"
Response from others	*"Well for a start there's your kids and your music, we're fed up with the noise they're making at night and not everyone likes your taste in music you know, we always have to live with it being your neighbours too!"*

(Continued)

6. Questions assertion	"Ok, anything else to add to the list before we make a start in resolving these issues?"
Response from others	*"Yes, can we add shopping to the list? We keep running out of stuff and I'm the one who spends most of my time replenishing it."*
7. Basic and Questions assertion	"Of course, let's now look to resolve each one at a time." "Shall we start with the money?"
Response from others	*"Ok, what did you have in mind?"*
8. Basic assertion	"When we've been out there's been a general reluctance to buy the first drinks, so we have. It's beginning to grate on us that nobody else is taking the lead."
Response from others	*"Yes, but we all chip in for any additional drinks we have with the meal'*
9. Basic assertion	"Yes, that's true but it's still us picking up the first tab."
Response from others	*"Oh, didn't know you felt this way, you should have said. Is there anything else to do with money that you're aggrieved about?"*
10. Basic and Questions assertion	"Well I'm not sure we give Anne and Greg enough money when they go to the shops?"
Response from others	*"Sometimes I put my own money in but it doesn't really matter it's only a few euros. It's the amount of time we spend shopping that's giving us a problem."*

11. Basic and Questions assertion	"That's a good example of us not sharing responsibilities."
	"With regards to money how about we make one person banker in charge of all expenditure and give them permission to ask each of us for the same amount when the kitty runs short?"
Response from others	*"That's a bit heavy isn't it, couldn't we all take it in turns?"*
12. Basic assertion	"Yes that's another way of doing it. It really doesn't matter as long as we all start sharing the load for not only the money but for the other things as well."
Response from others	*"I think the banker idea is the best one, let's go with that."*
We then begin to discuss the other matters in a spirit of mutual sharing.	

Praise the behaviour you want

Congratulate yourself for stepping out of your comfort zone; nobody likes confronting friends and neighbours. The risk may seem daunting but the dividends are huge. On occasions like this you might reward everyone with a glass of wine!

The more we face up to these challenges, the quicker we feel in control of our destiny, and not beholden to others and resentful towards those who appear to take the lead without consulting us first.

Time to choose

Now think about a situation of your own and write yourself an action plan based on the following questions:

- What specifically are you going to do?
- When will you start it?
- What might be potential barriers to stop you doing it?
- What aspects of this book can help you most in overcoming potential barriers?
- Whose help do you need to support you?
- How will you reward yourself?

11
Getting the Service You Deserve

Standing up for your own needs so that others acknowledge them

A real-life story

You're feeling fraught and overwhelmed at the moment; they say disasters come in threes.

1. A week ago your father was admitted to hospital with chest pain. You've made several visits but haven't yet managed to speak to anyone who can tell you what the problem is.

   On a number of occasions you've approached the nursing staff to ask questions about what's happening.

   Your questions have been met with an averted gaze, a rustle of paperwork and you're told that he's comfortable. You tried to speak to the consultant, who has always been unavailable; you have been given his number and told when he might be available to speak.

2. Meanwhile, your daughter's seventh birthday party planned for this afternoon is under jeopardy because your builders have let you down yet again. They promised to return this morning to re-connect the services they damaged yesterday. The only contact from them so far was an early morning call to say they had to go to another urgent job but would be back later, no time specified.

3. You've had to take a taxi to the hospital today because your car is yet again in the garage with an "intermittent" fault. It is the third time in three weeks it's been in the garage and now apparently it needs special expertize to resolve the problem. They have asked you to leave it with them for a few days to run some special tests but this now leaves you with transport problems.

You sit down and reflect over a cup of coffee, "why does this always happen to me?"

Wake-up call

Is this happening more and more frequently?

- The incidents where you accept what others tell you without challenging are increasing.
- Delays in the building work are mounting.
- Other people are being reactive towards you, not proactive.
- Others' priorities are seen to first.
- You have to get angry to get others' attention.
- You have to follow up all the time.
- You feel drained of energy.
- You're becoming less trusting of others.
- You feel like you can't achieve things and make things happen.
- You feel like you are "the problem" when you complain.
- No one provides you with information unless you ask for it.

Standing in the other person's shoes

What might others be saying to themselves?

- "Don't they realize we're doing our best?"
- "If we had any news we'd tell them."
- "We have enough to do in our job without having to keep everyone else informed."
- "They're not the only priority."
- "If they had real problems they'd shout louder."
- "We're wanting to help, but we're strapped for resources."
- "It's not the end of the world if these people have to wait another day."
- "They're not going to kick up a fuss so I can keep them waiting."

Taking things on when they're small

What in the past have you allowed to happen? Does any of this sound familiar?

- You accept second best as being ok.
- You allow people to easily ignore you – in all kinds of situations.
- You put other people's needs before yours.
- You allow people to fob you off.
- You tolerate being kept waiting.
- You become complicit with poor service and poor quality products.
- You accept the status quo.
- You avoid upsetting people and causing a fuss.

 ## Options

What mindset would be helpful?

- "It's my responsibility to get better service."
- "I can challenge the status quo."
- "I can make things happen."
- "I can get to the bottom of what's going on."
- "I can keep calm if there's an awkward exchange."
- "I can let them see that I'm serious and committed to finding a solution."
- "I can challenge them if they make excuses and find out the real reasons."
- "I can stand my ground and not be overlooked."
- "I can be respectful in my dealings with others and get them to respect my needs."
- "I can be clear and tell people how I feel and what I want."

What permission do you need to give yourself to tackle these situations assertively?

- I have the right to ask them to keep their promises.
- I have a right to persist.
- I have a right to get answers.
- I have the right to be treated with respect.
- I have the right to be listened to.
- I have the right to a response.
- I have the right for my needs to be taken seriously.
- I have the right to be kept informed.

What win-win outcomes are possible?

- The relatives are kept informed: the hospital receives good customer/patient feedback.
- I waste less time: they save on money, time and resources.
- I'm less fraught: my whole family benefit.
- I receive good quality service: they keep me as a loyal customer.
- My job is completed satisfactorily: I'm able to recommend them to others.
- I communicate in an authentic and honest way: others have the opportunity to change or correct something and improve their service in the future.

 Actions

If you want any situation to work out the way you want it to you need to take responsibility for that part of the situation you can influence.

When you receive bad service or accept poor quality and do nothing about it, nothing will change. Without challenge and feedback people may believe that they are providing adequate services or products.

So, it is your right and responsibility to challenge poor products and services. The win-win in these contexts is that you get value for your money and the service provider has an opportunity to put things right, retain customers and remain in business.

Only 4% of dissatisfied customers complain, yet bad news travels fast. Unhappy customers will tell upwards of 12 other people, and it costs five times more money and effort to attract new customers than it does to retain old ones.

Sadly, most dissatisfied customers will complain (behave non-assertively) to anyone and everyone except the person who can do something about it.

If you challenge bad service, the chances are that you will receive a far better service next time.

You can challenge assertively with calmness and integrity whilst maintaining the same courtesy to others. Challenging assertively will get things done and bring about change, futile complaining or whining won't.

In the three scenarios illustrated in the story we look at how to use assertive options to bring about change and achieve what you want.

During the conversation with hospital staff
This is where saying "no' assertively and the *verbal handshake* can be very effective.

1. Basic and Questions assertion	"Good morning, I want to organize a time to speak to my father's consultant face to face this week. I've tried to reach him by phone but he's always unavailable. What's the best way of going about this?"
Response from Nursing staff	*"Mr Cartwright is very busy, you could try his secretary, here's the number."*

(Continued)

211

2. Basic and Questions assertion	"Good morning, my father is being cared for on Westcott Ward and his consultant is Mr Cartwright, I'd like to organize a meeting with him to discuss my father's health."
Response from secretary	*"Mr Cartwright is very busy, can I give him a message and I'll get back to you with his response'*
3. Basic and Questions assertion and use of the "no" sandwich	"I appreciate that he's busy and it's difficult for him to find the time to speak directly with relatives. "No, this is very important and I'd like to speak with him myself in person. "When would be convenient for him and I'll make myself available?"
Response from secretary	*"Well he's in surgery all day today and then at a conference on Thursday and Friday. Can this wait until next week?"*
4. Basic and Questions assertion and use of the "no" sandwich	"I understand his diary is pretty packed. "No, I'm not prepared to wait until next week because the longer the delay the more anxious my mother and my family are becoming and I don't want this to continue. "When could he fit me in today?"
Resistance from secretary	*"Well I can't make time where there isn't time."*
5. Basic and Questions assertion and verbal handshake	"I appreciate it's difficult for you. "Do you accept that my family have received no confirmed diagnosis and that we're worried sick?"
Resistance from secretary	*"Yes of course I do. "Well I'm sure there's a good reason for the delay, I'll make contact with him between surgery and I'll promise to get back to you with a time to meet up by 2pm today."*

During the conversation with your builders

This is where use of the *verbal handshake* can be very effective.

1. Basic assertion and Questions assertion	"Steve, I want to talk with you about the impact of delays to our building work. "Can we do that now?"
Response from builder	*"Look, I'm sorry about this morning but we had an urgent call from a mate working on another customer's job and I couldn't say no."*
2. Empathy assertion/ verbal handshake	"I understand you want to try to keep all customers happy. "Can you see the problems you caused for me and my daughter's party when you failed to turn up this morning?"
Resistance from builder	*" Yes I can, but if I'd not helped out the other customer they'd have gone mad."*
3. Basic and Questions assertion	"In future I'd like you prioritize my job until the work's completed. "How do you feel about this?"
Resistance from builder	*"Yes, but some customers won't listen when you tell them you can't just drop everything."*
4. Discrepancy assertion	" Steve, you told me at the start that you would be working full time on my extension, now you're telling me you have other obligations that may affect the progress of this work. "I want to return to our original agreement and for you to stay focused on this project." "Can you accept this?"

Assertiveness

During the conversation with the garage

This is where use of the *"no" sandwich* and the *verbal handshake* can be very effective.

1. Questions assertion	"Please can I have the use of a courtesy car whilst you're running tests on mine?"
Response from garage	*"Sorry, we've only a few and they're all booked out."*
2. Empathy assertion/verbal handshake	"I can see the problem you have with so few courtesy cars. "Can you see the difficulty I'm caused because I'm left without transport while you have my car?"
Response from garage	*"Well yes, sorry, but if you want your car fixed you've got to leave it with us."*
3. "No" sandwich	"I appreciate the efforts you're making to fix my car. "No, I'm not prepared to wait any longer without the use of a courtesy car. "How can we go about organizing one for next week?"
Resistance from garage	*"I just said, we don't have many and they're all booked out to people who are having annual services."*
4. Basic assertion	"Each time you return my car you tell me you think it's now fixed. However the fault continues. "On the three previous occasions you didn't offer a car I think it's reasonable that I should have one now."
Resistance from garage	*"I can see you're point and would like to help, but I don't have a courtesy car available at the moment. Leave it with me and I'll see what I can do. I'll get back to you by 4pm today."*

Praise the behaviour you want

When you get acceptance of your requests and even a positive response, congratulate yourself for stepping out of your comfort zone. Nobody likes complaining, but if you don't stand up for your needs, nobody else will.

You appreciate praise and recognition for a job well done. Generally there is not much praise given to those working in the service industry. Success can often be measured in the absence of problems, i.e. "no complaints this week," or "we achieved fewer than three rejects" and so on. There are departments for customer complaints none for customer success; praise is not often sprinkled around.

When an individual or a company gives excellent customer service it is important to praise the behaviour and say how specifically it has helped. You will be remembered, for you will be in the minority and you can imagine the service you will receive the next time when you return.

 ## Time to choose

Now think about a situation of your own and write yourself an action plan based on the following questions:

- What specifically are you going to do?
- · When will you start it?
- What might be potential barriers to stop you doing it?
- What aspects of this book can help you most in overcoming potential barriers?
- Whose help do you need to support you?
- How will you reward yourself?

Sustaining Your Assertion

*Maintain your self-confidence
and well-being*

If you were one of those people who are permanently high on self-belief, confidence and self-esteem, you would have no need to pick up a book like this.

For the rest of us it can be a chicken and egg situation because, in order to be more assertive, we need to feel self-confident and empowered and, in order to become more self-empowered, we need to be more assertive!

We have, throughout the book, chosen to concentrate on the latter option.

Even if we don't feel self-confident and high on self-esteem, knowing and understanding the beliefs and practices of assertion and behaving "as if" you were . . . will increase your self-confidence and esteem because you will be successful in what you do.

Each time you behave assertively, with commitment, you will affirm your assertiveness because you amass more and more evidence that your assertion works. You increase your capacity to productively handle the challenges around you.

We believe, like Stephen Covey in his outstanding book, *The Seven Habits of Highly Effective People* – who talks about "sharpening the saw" – that you need to renew your resources, energy and health to create a sustainable, *balanced*, long-term, assertive life style.

A colleague of ours, Sandra Crathern, a gifted and successful life coach, uses a tool she calls "The Health Fountain." Sandra walks the talk, and the health fountain comes from her own experience.

The health fountain

About her health fountain, Sandra says, "just acknowledging the reality of your true feelings is a very good place to start.

"I put together my health fountain to point people in the right direction, to show them where to look to evaluate how they were feeling."

If you look at the health fountain you can see elements which are common to everyone. These elements are a part of each and every person's life, and the fountain will give you a visual representation of your life and whether you have *balance*.

The health fountain is split into two areas, the tangible and the non-tangible.

Innavision

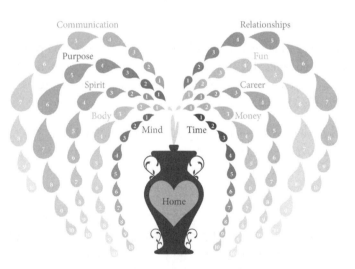

Health Fountain
Respect your health. *From the inside out.*

Health Fountain reproduced with permission of Sandra Crathern

How to use the fountain

Look at the fountain and start by thinking about yourself, and how you feel inside. The middle of the fountain represents you and your home.

You will see that each of the elements is numbered from 1 to 10. Put a ring around the number which represents how you feel about that element:

1. You are not feeling very happy about this in your life.
10. You are feeling very happy about that element in your life.

An interpretation of the elements

- **Internal communication.** How effectively do you listen to your own body, when you need to eat, sleep, rest or do you ignore your body's signals?
- **External communication.** How effectively do you communicate your needs to others? Are you able to effectively and *honestly* communicate?
- **Purpose.** Do you feel that you have a purpose? Do you feel you know what it is? How do you feel about your purpose?
- **Body.** Do you take care of your body? Are you in good health? Do you respect your body? Do you overeat, smoke, or drink too much? Do you take regular exercise?
- **Spirit.** Spirituality is a very personal concept and means so much and such different things to different people. But I believe that having a sense of spirit or belief is a key aspect of life. Finding a sense of spirit can be comforting.
- **Mind.** Do you feel balanced in your mind? Are you optimistic or pessimistic – is the glass half empty or half full?
- **Relationships.** The first thing to mention is that when we talk about relationships we are not talking about whether you have a relationship with a partner but relationships in general, and relationships that are important to you. If you

don't have a relationship of any importance, you may want
to acknowledge you feelings in this area.

- **Fun.** Plain and simple, do you have fun? Do you remember
the last time you had fun?
- **Career.** Again, you may or may not have a career but you
need to broaden your thoughts. A career could be where you
spend most of your time, your job, or how you feel about a
career if you do not have one.
- **Money.** Unfortunately, in today's society, money does feature
in our lives. Do you have a healthy attitude towards money?
Do you have enough or too little? Do you save too much
and it impacts on other areas of your life?
- **Time management.** How do you manage your time? Do you
manage your time effectively for you, your life and what you
need to fit in to your life? Do you feel you waste time or are
continually late?
- **Personal time.** Do you make enough time for yourself? How
does time impact on your life?

The health fountain is a very subjective tool and it is for you to
interpret in relation to your own life and use the elements and suggestions as a guide. Your interpretations of each of the elements is
more important than the suggestions listed above.

The scores are not important, it's a visual tool to look at the *balance*
in your life. This should not be used to judge your life, it is designed
to help you evaluate how you feel about your life.

Looking at your health fountain and your scores, how do you feel
about them overall? Do you have *balance*? What do you notice
about your health fountain?

The most important question you need to ask yourself now is: if
nothing changes within the next 2–3 years is that OK?

If you are looking at your health fountain, and evaluating how you feel about it, I am sure that something will jump out at you, whether it is the area with the lowest score or just something that is more prevalent to you that you feel needs to be given more attention in your life.

Let's spend a few moments thinking about the "fun" element in life. This is something which, as we all get older and take on more responsibilities, can be lost. It's very hard to put your finger on until you see a visual representation of your life, such as the health fountain, which may demonstrate that actually this is an area of your life that doesn't score highly (although I would like to reiterate that the number of your score overall is not important).

Fun itself is key to having a healthy, happy *balance* in your life and, without fun to lighten your heart and your soul, your life may feel empty. For example, if you can introduce just a little more fun, automatically you would feel more energized, more positive, your mood would be enhanced, you would probably start to feel less tense, respond to others more positively and as a result other people's reactions to you would be noticeably different, the effects go on and you would then go on to see different sides of people that you may not have seen before.

The key is to change something, and small changes can make the most profound difference. There will be a knock-on effect throughout all the elements of your life when you make any small, simple changes. It is important not to look at your whole visual life picture (your health fountain) and try to change everything, or imagine that changing everything is a task outside your reach, as it will become overwhelming.

We have enjoyed talking to you, through the medium of this book, about the benefits of being assertive and becoming the architect of your own realities.

Together, we have looked at how you:

- Communicate your ideas, opinions and feelings both verbally and non-verbally, clearly and confidently, building relationships on the basis of mutual respect.
- Reinforce your own sense of self-esteem and worth and negotiate in a way that achieves outcomes that are good for you and others, achieving the best possible outcome.
- Maintain your assertion when circumstances become tough without stepping into aggressive or non-assertive behaviours, resolving difficult situations in a spirit of win-win.
- Underpin your assertion by developing enabling beliefs, removing those that inhibit your growth and success in life.
- Listen to the endless chatter that goes on inside your head, distinguishing those internal debates that are positively harmful and replacing them with helpful and enabling self-talk.
- Give yourself permission, through assertive rights, to act in self-empowering ways both for you and others.
- Implement these tools and techniques into the many areas of your life and know what action to take to resolve tricky situations with greater elegance and positive effect.
- Sustain your assertive behaviour and maintain your well-being by looking after yourself, so you can attain greater fulfilment and enjoy the life you deserve.

So, are you ready to make a change and become more assertive?

One ounce of action is greater than one ton of theory.
Friedrich Engels

About the Authors

Conrad and Suzanne Potts have been motivational speakers, management trainers and coaches for over 25 years. They have appeared in a number of TV programmes and training videos associated with assertiveness, team building and leadership.

Over the last twenty five years Conrad and Suzanne have helped literally thousands of people increase their confidence and lead more fulfilling and successful lives.

They have delivered assertiveness training around the world working with people from diverse cultures from Pakistan to Paris, Sydney to Stockholm and Moscow to Manchester.

Conrad and Suzanne have found the core messages of assertiveness resonate as loudly in the boardroom as they do in the bedroom.

Both are founder members of TeamSkills; a network of management and leadership consultants dedicated to the development of individual and corporate excellence.

We're also curious to know how this book has helped you so please feel free to contact our blog at www.teamskills.co.uk.

Photo reproduced with permission of Clive Strotten (Clive Strotten Photography)

Acknowledgements

We thank all those people who have attended our courses and who have given us stories, anecdotes and examples of how assertion has changed their lives. We have been inspired by the humility and courage of people who have not accepted the status quo and have ignored, "It'll never work", or "that can't be done", who have got out there and made it happen and expressed themselves with clarity, honesty and calmness.

We will always be grateful to our original assertiveness gurus, Ken & Kate Back for educating us in the things they believed in and practised.

Finally, thanks to Sandra Crathern for her input on health & well-being.

Index